Claude Monet at Giverny

A Tour and History of the House and Garden

Claire Joyes

Éditions Claude Monet Giverny

"Apart from painting and gardening, I'm good for nothing!"

Claude Monet

*"Sometimes I went to sit on the bench from which Monet
saw so much in the reflections of his water garden.
Only with perseverance could my untrained eye follow
the Master's brush even distantly to the extreme limits
of his revelations."*

Georges Clemenceau

*Monet used to watch the changing light on the water lilies from the bench beside the pond,
shown here in a photograph taken by Nickolas Muray in 1926.*

"Monday 30 October

Set off early this morning for Giverny. Rain all day.
Mr Monet showed us his cathedrals. There are twenty-six
of them, magnificent, some all in shades of violet,
others in whites, yellows, with a blue sky, others in pinks
with a slightly green sky, some in fog, two or three
in shade below and with shafts of sunshine lighting
the towers. These cathedrals, admirably well drawn
and massive, are yet so soaring and you can decipher
every detail. It seems so hard to me not to draw in
all the details.

These paintings by Mr Monet are a good lesson in
painting. The house has changed since we were last
at Giverny. Mr Monet has had a bedroom made
for himself above the studio, with large windows,
doors and floor in pitch pine, with white hangings.
There are many paintings in this bedroom, including
Isabelle Combing her Hair, *Gabrielle with a Bowl*
and *Cocotte with a Hat*, a pastel by Maman, a pastel
by Uncle Edouard, a very pretty nude by Mr Renoir,
some Pissarros etc.

Mme Monet's bedroom has blue wainscoting, those
of Mlles Blanche and Germaine have violet. We did
not see Mlle Marthe's bedroom. Mlle Blanche showed
us some of her paintings, with pretty colouring,
two of trees reflected in the Epte resembling
M. Monet's paintings.

The sitting room has violet woodwork, lots of Japanese
engravings on the walls, as well as in the dining room
which is all yellow. We walked beneath some poplars
to the greenhouse, where there are some magnificent
chrysanthemums. Then the lake, which has a green
bridge in Japanese style."

Diary of Julie Manet, 1893.

Right:
Claude Monet, step-grandfather, holding Sisi in his arms, around 1904.

Contents

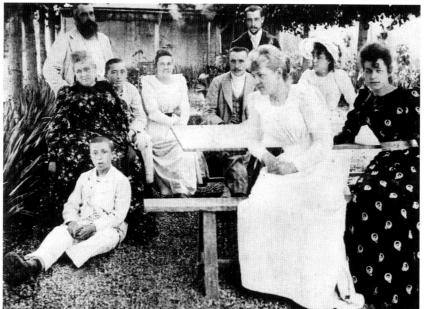

Family History

Claude Monet photographed by
Theodore Robinson, around 1887.

Clockwise from left:

Alice Hoschedé (during the Rottembourg years).

*Four Hoschedé children
(during the Rottembourg years).*

*Ernest Hoschedé
(during the Rottembourg years).*

*James Butler (Jim) as a child in the blue sitting
room at Giverny.*

*Lily Butler taking a photograph of
Monet smoking one of his eternal cigarettes
at the entrance to the studio-sitting room.*

*A photograph by Theodore Robinson of the
family under the lime trees in around 1890,
showing (clockwise from left) Claude Monet
and Jacques Hoschedé, Alice, Jean-Pierre
Hoschedé, Blanche Hoschedé, Jean Monet,
Germaine (Maine) Hoschedé, Michel Monet,
Marthe Hoschedé, Suzanne Hoschedé.*

Maine and Marthe on the veranda.

It is impossible to disentangle the complexities of the Monet-Hoschedé family without going back a little in time, to events that may have seemed insignificant at the time, but which turned out to have momentous repercussions. So it was that, one day in 1876, Ernest Hoschedé invited Monet to come and paint at his house, the Château de Rottembourg at Montgéron. No one could then have known that the rotunda drawing room at Rottembourg would lead eventually to the studio-sitting room at Giverny.

Ernest Hoschedé was a wealthy merchant dealing in luxury fine linen, elegant shawls and Indian cashmeres, who on his father's death found himself managing partner of the prosperous firm of Hoschedé-Blemont, founded in 1736. For the Exposition Universelle of 1867 he had commissioned his own pavilion from the fashionable architect Paul Sédille, in which to offer a tastefully elegant display of the articles purveyed by the firm. The pavilion did not go unnoticed, and was the subject of two engravings in the exhibition catalogue.

If truth be told, however, the world of commerce held no interest for Ernest, whose only true passion was art. A collector of longstanding, he was a pioneer in buying "modern art", adding works by Courbet, Degas and Monet (whom he did not yet know) to his collection of paintings by Corot, Boudin and others. He was lavish in his purchases, much to the despair of his mother, who wrote wearily in her diary: "My son has not been seen in the shop for a week now, he must have spent every day at the Louvre."

Against his parents' wishes Ernest married Alice Raingo, a young woman of considerable fortune from a family of bronze-founders and clockmakers to the courts of Europe. Her generous dowry from her father included the gift of the Château de Rottembourg at Montgéron; there she loved to spend as much time as possible, perpetually delaying her return to Paris. Ernest and Alice had five children and a sixth on the way when their affairs started to go badly awry.

Spoilt and self-indulgent as they were, they lived in a social whirl of dinners and parties, sometimes chartering special train to convey their guests to the chateau. Their friends included a number of artists, and their friend and neighbour Carolus-Duran was always on their guest list. They would also invite artists such as Manet and Sisley to come and paint in the country, though Manet – never happier than when he was in society – could not endure the party atmosphere at Montgeron for long (perhaps especially as life in the country held few attractions for him).

The highly cultivated Hoschedé was shrewd in his collecting – though not financially, as he invariably paid the asking price for his paintings and never attempted to beat the price down, a trait sufficiently rare to be worthy of comment. Buyers and *soi-disant* patrons of art too numerous to mention have always seized on every opportunity to take advantage of impecunious artists, buying works at rock-bottom prices when they are well aware of their probable future importance and – an inevitable side-effect of this glorious destiny – their value on the art market. But by now Hoschedé's extravagance was beginning to undermine his finances. He sold paintings in any event in order to ring the changes in his collections, but refused to heed the clear warnings from his first sale, buying and selling with no regard to chronology. In this world of the initiated, of dealers, collectors and artists, people tended to assume that such sales were examples of strategic speculation, when in fact they were genuine lapses of judgement that would in the end prove fatal, financial contortions that were nothing more than symptoms of collapse.

Incorrigible and impenitent, by 1876 Hoschedé was a man living on borrowed time who brazenly hung his walls with *The Arrival of the Normandy Train* and two other *Gare Saint-Lazare* paintings by Monet, from whom he also commissioned four large decorative canvases for the rotunda drawing room at Rottembourg. At liberty to choose his own subjects, Monet painted *Turkeys at the Château de Rottembourg, Corner of the Garden at Rottembourg, The Lake at Rottembourg* and *The Hunt*.

By now financial ruin was knocking at his door. From his sales he kept back only his Impressionist paintings, his only purchase a Bartholdi sculpture. When the fall finally came it was swift and terrible. On 15 May 1878 Rottembourg was sold at a knock-down price, along with its furniture and orange trees. In mid-June, 117 paintings followed suit. The *Corner of the Garden at Rottembourg* and *The Lake at Rottembourg* went to Russia, where they enriched the Morosov collection.

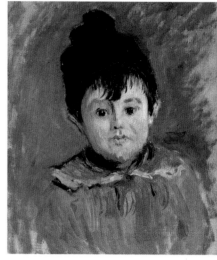

Claude Monet, Michel Monet in a Bobble Hat, *1880, Musée Marmottan-Monet, Paris.*

The long catalogue of horrors attendant on financial ruin was endless and unbearable, and the Hoschedé family, who had become friends with the Monet family in Paris, took refuge with them at Vétheuil. Now it was the penniless Monets who offered hospitality to the Hoschedés. But further disgrace lay in store for Ernest: sentenced to a month's imprisonment, he managed to escape to Belgium, which allowed entry to bankrupts. On his return to France he frequented the same salons and resumed his friendships with Forain, Charles Cros, Mallarmé and Suzanne and Edouard Manet, among others. He became an art critic, and in 1880 founded a sumptuous review entitled *L'Art et la Mode*, in which Mallarmé would publish his *Nénufar Blanc (White Waterlily)*.

Ernest Hoschedé's failings, his fatal tendency to act like a spoilt child and bury his head in the sand, and his blithe lack of any sense of responsibility, should not blind us to the fact, however, that he was also a man of exceptional culture, a true benefactor to artists, and a gifted collector of dozens of masterpieces now scattered among the world's most prestigious museums. This was the man who was the first if all-too-fleeting owner of *Impression, Sunrise*, of whom Daniel Wildenstein was to observe a century later, "Hoschedé had a good eye, he should have been art dealer." Which is no mean compliment.

Sadly, Hoschedé was never able to put together another collection. Once again, as at Montgéron, he was more often in Paris than in the country at Vétheuil. At this point the rift between Alice and Ernest became unbridgeable. Both households, the Monets and the Hoschedés, were shattered: the Monet family by the cruel and painful death of the exquisite Camille Monet, struck down in the full bloom of youth and nursed devotedly and in genuine friendship by Alice and her eldest daughter Marthe; the Hoschedés by Ernest's ruin and his inability to provide for his family's needs. Put bluntly, it was only by sponging off the Monets that the Hoschedés were able to survive on such straitened means. Ernest attempted to sell Monet's paintings in Paris,

Claude Monet, Michel Monet as a Child, *n.d., Musée Marmottan-Monet, Paris.*

without any great success and against a general background of political and financial crisis. Durand-Ruel was the first to feel the tragic consequences of this harsh climate, which only added to the general lack of enthusiasm for the new painting.

Paradoxically, however, this period of real physical privation for all at Vétheuil had one positive effect: prodigious in his output as never before, Monet worked as though his life depended on it, producing a series of what may justifiably be called masterpieces. Faced with the contrast between the courage of this artist fighting with all his strength in the teeth of adversity on the one hand, and on the other the fecklessness and irresponsibility of her own husband, on whom she could not even depend for sensible advice, Alice made a momentous personal choice: she would bring up Monet's two children (especially Michel, still a toddler when his mother died) with her own. Deeply pious by nature, even to the point of mystic fervour, she was profoundly affected by the censure of society at large and of her own family, while struggling painfully with her own moral and religious dilemmas. In making this agonized choice between Monet, whom she viewed with an admiration that eventually turned to love, and her duty to return to the side of a husband who had after all abandoned her when she was expecting their sixth child, Jean-Pierre, Alice displayed a remarkable strength of character. And what was to be done, after all, about the Monet children of whom she had grown so fond? In reality, the household now consisted of six Hoschedé children and two little Monets. They moved from Vétheuil to Poissy, which they chose because the children could go to school there and it was close to Paris, so solving the two eternal problems. It was at Poissy that the crisis stirred up by this unconventional arrangement came to a head.

While Ernest and Alice had been irresponsible, they could never have been described as morally lax in any way. Monet for his part was scrupulously honourable, the very antithesis of a free-living bohemian – a bourgeois family man who

Claude Monet, Les deux petits *(Michel Monet and Jean-Pierre Hoschedé), 1881, Musée Marmottan-Monet, Paris.*

was already deeply attached to his "adoptive" children. Monet and Hoschedé made a pact. Clearly divorce was unthinkable, so they agreed a compromise that was clear and dignified – though Hoschedé was to have difficulty in respecting its terms. Monet was unambiguous when he wrote to him from Poissy on 1 January 1883:

> *Allow me to tell you how painful it is for me to think that my very presence prevents you from being with your children today. I had hoped that my going away for a few days would have persuaded you to consent to come and spend New Year's Day with them; you have refused to give them this happiness. I am deeply sorry for this, as in previous years you have not acted so.*
>
> *Yet if I am in the midst of your family is this not by common accord, and was it not with your agreement that I rented our house at Poissy? Yes, you know very well that it was, yet you have suddenly decided not to come here any more, and you have created an extremely difficult situation between ourselves.*
>
> *For this reason, although I am well aware that a letter from me will be no more agreeable to you than the sight of me, I cannot restrain myself from telling you of my sadness.*
>
> *Claude Monet*

Very soon Poissy became *"l'horrible Poissy"*, and they had to leave. Monet found it difficult to work there, and problems seemed to multiply on all fronts: they were constantly ill, and the famous flood that delighted the children stretched their parents' nerves to breaking point. To crown it all they were short of money, and Monet was forced to send begging letters to friends, buyers and above all Paul Durand-Ruel, who was himself in serious difficulties. Well aware both of Monet's worries and

Claude Monet and Peggy Hart ready to go out in an open carriage, around 1898.

Tea on the front steps, served by Blanche. The party includes (from left to right) Alice (half-obscured), Suzanne in a hat, Blanche standing and Claude Monet, around 1898.

Shown walking to the pond are (from left to right) Madame Kuroki, Claude Monet, Lily Butler, Blanche Hoschedé-Monet and Georges Clemenceau (photograph taken by M. Kuroki in June 1921).

Claude Monet photographed by Sacha Guitry in 1913.

despondency and of his ability to weather storms of every kind, the eminent dealer seems to have been the only person to offer practical advice and common sense:

Paris, 26 May 1882

My dear Monsieur Monet

… "if your house at Poissy brings unhappiness to you and ill-health to you and your family, there is a simple remedy. Leave it and move elsewhere. It is better to lose a few months' rent than your health. Do not worry if you incur a financial loss. Paint lots of paintings, and good ones, and both of us will earn enough to keep the landlords at bay."

Durand-Ruel

No sooner said than done: Monet decided to leave, seeking advice from Pissarro in September 1882:

My dear friend

May I ask you for some information about the school at Pontoise?… on the subject of Pontoise, is it easy to find a house and garden there, on the outskirts, about twenty minutes outside town?

It would not be strictly accurate to say that Monet chose Giverny, of which he had a vague idea, perhaps from some distant memory. At this period people travelled on foot and by boat, and the Seine was both far busier with traffic and – it is tempting to say – more cherished than it is nowadays. In 1868, Monet had spent some time with Camille and their son Jean on the Ile de Gloton, near Bonnières, a village recommended by Zola, who had been there with Cézanne; later on, from their base at Vétheuil, where they loved to go on family boat trips up and down the river, Monet would doubtless have visited Vernon. This was where he decided to use the little train on the line between Pacy-sur-Eure and Gisors as his base for a systematic exploration of the villages in the area.

At Giverny he discovered a natural landscape of luxuriance and beauty, a pristine rural scene of houses dotted between fields, large vegetable gardens beside the river, rich pastures cropped by well-fed cows, mixed hedgerows, traditional hedges charmingly pruned, little bridges over streams and old stone wash-houses.

Luck would need to be on his side if he was to find a house, as time was not on his side. The lease at Poissy was due to run out at the end of April. Then one day he returned triumphant at last. Those who witnessed the move, which took a fortnight, must have wondered if they were seeing things. Though they had little money, the family boasted no fewer than four boats: the studio boat reminiscent of Daubigny's *Bottin*, which Monet had already at Argenteuil, two mahogany skiffs and *la norvégienne*, a broad, flat-bottomed rowing boat.

On 29 April Paul Durand-Ruel received another desperate appeal:

My dear Monsieur Durand

Our move is not yet over. For the past week I have had nothing but problems. Tomorrow, finally, I leave for Giverny with some of the children. But we are so short of money that Madame Hoschedé cannot go, and she must leave the house before ten o'clock tomorrow morning. I beg you, therefore, to give the bearer of this letter one or two notes of a hundred francs, whatever you can manage, and to send the same to me directly at Giverny, by Vernon, Eure, as we shall be penniless there…

Further appeals for funds followed, as there was no time to be lost in building a barn at l'Ile-aux-Orties on the Seine to provide shelter for his boats, canvases and easels. But these newcomers setting up home in the village were *horsins*, strangers to Normandy and to Giverny, and were thus to be treated with suspicion. And an artist to boot! How bizarre! That wasn't a *real* job. But this was only the beginning for the people of Giverny. Though the countryside was delightful, the villagers were rather less so, and the Hoschedé-Monets found themselves the victims of a veritable campaign of persecution.

During their nomadic lives, Claude Monet and Alice Hoschedé had between them lived in an extravagantly eclectic range of buildings and architectural styles, from the Hôtel d'Epernon on rue Vieille du Temple, rue des Petites-Ecuries and boulevard Haussmann in Paris to the Château de Rottembourg, the Villa Marie at Biarritiz, two delightful houses at Argenteuil, cramped and wretched Vétheuil and the Villa Saint-Louis at "ghastly Poissy", where their last days had been blighted by tumultuous floodwaters that had forced them to take refuge on the first floor and to navigate the ground floor by boat, while the terrified servants fled. And now there was this altogether less menacing but still rather odd bourgeois house that he had decided to buy in 1890.

Monet and Anna on the recently built Japanese bridge.

Claude Monet, On the Beach at Trouville, *1870-1, Musée Marmottan-Monet, Paris. The figures are unidentified young relatives of Camille.*

When Monet wrote to Duret and Pissarro, "I am in raptures, Giverny is a splendid region for me", rhapsodizing on the "magnificent country", he was speaking as an artist, thinking only of the landscape; the lakes and marshes; a dense carpet of wild iris; two hills that were so different, the one all inlets planted with apricot trees and cornfields, with a sea of poppies, the other wooded, steep, sheer and vertical, dark and often tinged with blue. He was not thinking of his own gloomy garden, nor of the architectural blandness of the house. Here his response was purely practical: the garden needed to be made, and that was all he asked. As for the house, it could be adapted to accommodate the whole tribe.

But what did Alice and her eldest child Marthe think of their new home, and of the society in which they now must mix? Who could they see, with whom could they converse or take tea during the long winters, when Monet was away on painting trips for months at a time? Their trials were not over, and financial ruin was not an easy thing to assimilate.

Monet meanwhile never gave up, laden down though he was with petty domestic problems and fears that he might have made the wrong choice. To Durand-Ruel he confided: "I feel I've been foolish in choosing to live so far out, I'm in despair about it…" He did not yet know that he could count on the valiant little train and on Gaston's horse and cart, that Paris – indispensable to all – with its exhibitions, dinners, friends, collectors and dealers, was only a stone's throw away from Giverny. Moreover the house was not Cézanne's Jas de Bouffan, nor Manet and Morisot's Le Mesnil, Renoir's Les Collettes or Caillebotte's Le Casin. None of these was truly an artist's house, as Giverny was to be – not a country house, but the house he lived in with his family. Charm was clearly going to be a prerequisite.

Claude Monet, Walking near Argenteuil, *1873, Musée Marmottan-Monet, Paris. The painting depicts Camille and Jean with a friend.*

The House

Curiously, this was the second pink house with green shutters in which Monet had lived (the first was at Argenteuil), and the second time his house had been separated from the garden by a road (as had also been the case at Vétheuil). At Giverny the railway also ran along the Chemin du Roy, parallel to the Ru, causing Clemenceau to remark one day, "He even has a railway in the garden."

Standing between two lanes, ruelle Leroy and ruelle l'Amsicourt, at the spot known as Le Pressoir, the house was in traditional rural style like its neighbours, north-facing and of modest proportions, with four rooms downstairs and up, flanked at one end by a single-storey barn and at the other by a store-room. It appeared to be the only house to rent, and given its position at the heart of the village it is more than likely that Monet would have forgotten about it, had it not been for its walled garden and generous grounds covering some two and a half acres. Over the years the old farmhouse had been "gentrified": its former owners, merchants from Guadeloupe, had given it a slate roof, an unusual feature in this region, and had broken the straight lines of the façade with a central Attic pediment, itself pierced with an *oeil-de-boeuf* window – all with a view to distracting from the solid country proportions of the pink ochre façade and its serried windows with grey shutters. A central flight of stone steps, meanwhile, led up to the half-glazed front door.

The gloomy garden, with no colour or flowers, was laid out to either side of a broad avenue of conifers leading down almost to the Chemin du Roy. Sombre and dark, it was devoid of poetry or imagination. It was all rather depressing, and hopelessly at odds with glorious countryside all around, with the extraordinary quality of the light in the dense bluish mists that hovered over the Epte and the Seine, the rare beauty of wetlands landscapes.

Time flew by. Monet had been living at Le Pressoir for over a month already, and between the problems to be seen to at Poissy, the demented business of moving their goods and chattels (partly by boat along the Seine), the death of Manet, the

The house façade.

The house façade smothered with Virginia creeper and roses.

need to house the boats securely and the business of moving in, it felt much longer since he last lifted a brush. But perhaps now he felt anchored, perhaps now his wanderings were over. Now at last he could get down to work.

On 5 June 1883, he wrote to Durand-Ruel:

> *Dear Monsieur Durand*
>
> *As soon as I have anything good I shall send it to you. Now I can concentrate only on painting, as I have been sorely distracted by the need to sort out my boats; as the Seine is some distance from the house I have had to find a way of storing them securely; then there's been the gardening that has rather absorbed me, so that I can cut a few flowers to paint on days when the weather is bad. At last all this is done.*

Then there was the appearance of the house to think of, which meant above all sorting out a studio, without further delay. Soon the house was enlarged with the addition of another floor on each side of the pediment. A broad wooden veranda ran the length of the façade, with glazed doors and french windows opening on to it from every room, so giving each its independence. The shutters were painted green. With its three flights of steps and its veranda widening into a central terrace on axis with the central avenue, the house had the charm of simplicity.

Many an elegant façade conceals disappointments within: impersonal drawing rooms, neglected libraries, regrettable carpets and paintings that are best passed over in silence. Giverny is quite the opposite: behind an unremarkable exterior lies an interior that could hardly be more fascinating. You climb a few steps, go in the front door – and the sheer unexpectedness of it all takes your breath away. You feel you have entered a different world, just as you do in the garden: the colours and comforts, though solidly bourgeois in their arrangement, are so astonishingly modern in feel. The dining room, blue sitting room and Epicerie (spice store) whisk you away to the England of Hogarth and above all to Japan. With its bold and original touches, this could only be an artist's house. Its classicism reflects Alice's tastes, but the colours are Monet's. Monet always had the final say. Once, when he was away on his travels, Alice wrote to tell him that she had changed her bedroom and altered the arrangement of the furniture, and that she was pleased with the result; Monet's reply was, "I'll have to wait and see."

Sometimes the logic behind the layout of old houses is not immediately apparent. Why, for instance, is the Epicerie reached from the blue sitting room and the studio-sitting room, rather then the kitchen? The answer is that in a house without corridors this room plays an essential role, as any room can become a passageway.

Guests arriving at Giverny could use a variety of routes, according to who they were and their reason for coming. Thus collectors and dealers who had come for lunch might pass through the Epicerie to go down to the studio, returning an hour later via the same route to the dining room, passing through the blue sitting room where the family would gather until the gong summoned them to table. With external steps leading directly up to it, the Epicerie was also the only way to reach the staircase leading to Monet's bedroom, which on days of despair, doubt and ill

The nasturtiums on the central path.

Top to bottom:

The central path, with relatives in mourning after the death of Ernest Hoschedé, 1891.

The central path, with the nasturtiums poised to invade.

The central path as Monet liked to walk down it three times a day.

humour meant that he could avoid encountering anybody. Sometimes he would spend several days at a stretch brooding in his room, during which time meals would be brought to him there and the house would be shrouded in silence – even the dining room, now that it was deserted by the master of the house.

The Epicerie played an important role, beneath the knowing gaze of the superb prints hanging on the walls, notably the five-panel Sadahide print showing European merchant ships with fluttering flags carrying goods from Yokohama to western ports and vice versa, and another print by the same artist showing ladies in kimonos and crinolines mingling together at the counters of foreign traders in Yokohama. The engravings with their predominantly blue tones share the room with a large bulbous-fronted armoire that was kept locked, under the exclusive jurisdiction of the mistress of the house. To her alone it offered an exotic voyage of discovery, as recalled by the presence of the Sadahide prints. The treasures it contained – heavy with the perfumes of Bourbon vanilla, nutmeg and cloves from Cayenne, cinnamon from Ceylon and pepper from the Dutch East Indies – were both rare and costly at this time. Packets from the famous Corcellet delicatessen gave off the aroma of coffee from Java; teas from India and Ceylon (China tea did not appear until the turn of the century) were stored in tins, sachets and boxes from Parisian specialists such as Hédiard, born under Napoleon III; Kardomah and the Compagnie Coloniale were also purveyors of teas, over which Britain exercised the monopoly. The finest London stores supplied scones, muffins and fudge, while Fortnum & Mason provided handsome fruit cakes and Christmas puddings. Almost as exotic were the bonbons from Fouquet in Paris, the Calissons d'Aix, the olive oil also from Aix, tins as big as hat boxes packed with foie gras from Alsace, Périgord truffles steeped in golden Armagnac and numerous other delicacies.

Life at Giverny was to unfold in the absence of Frédéric Bazille and of Manet, who died on the day Monet arrived there, without the too-brief friendship of Berthe Morisot and Caillebotte, for young Jean without the presence of his mother Camille, and for Marthe with the incomprehensibly irregular appearances of her father Ernest, so difficult to predict. As in every other family, a succession of great joys and tragedies bound them tightly together, and Monet – who never spoke of his almost certainly unhappy childhood – worried over the children, kept a close eye on their studies and shared their games. When Suzanne married Theodore Butler, he was determined to lead her to the altar as Alice's lawful husband, taking the place of Ernest who had died a year earlier. A complete paterfamilias, he was the undisputed patriarch of the house.

Neither he nor Alice thought of their life as provincial. They lived in the country, which was altogether different. Hence the walled garden. Eventually they forged relationships with true local country families, but it would take time before their hens started to lay, their cows gave sufficient milk and their blackcurrant bushes bore fruit.

Monet was by nature distant and reserved. For Alice, more open and spontaneously friendly by temperament, the dash of snobbery in her character – which had stubbornly persisted through all the vicissitudes of their lives together – must have made life more complicated. Her social contacts were made after mass, to which she went with the children, alongside with those who fancied themselves as the local notables, and who took care to snub any artists. Which was perhaps just as well, as they would have had little to say to each other. Although helped by servants, even at the beginning of their time at Giverny, and by her older daughters Marthe, Blanche and Suzanne (Maine was still too young and away at school), Alice had her work cut out at Giverny; what kept her going was her role as mother, a role that she was resolved to fulfil to the best of her ability. Running a household wasn't easy, and someone had to keep tabs on everyone's little extravagances.

Alice loved the country, and at Rottembourg she had been used to being a hostess, to filling the house with crowds of friends. But all that was in the past. Still, the proximity of Paris was an essential factor not only for Monet but also for Alice: friends were always eager to come, though perhaps less so in winter. And winter was precisely the time when Monet decided to take off on his "painting trips", the dead season when there was nothing left to do in the garden and he needed to restore his flagging energies. If his travels took him far he might be away for as much as three months. These were the hardest times for Alice, when she waited with impatience for the post, or for parcels of flowers or shells, or for almost anything else: fabrics, wickerwork, local gastronomic specialities or plants for the garden. Mandarins from Bordighera, mimosa from Menton, lobsters from Belle-Ile or furs from Norway: almost anything was possible. Monet was a prolific letter-writer, too, bombarding the family with advice and suggestions of every kind, often addressed particularly to Blanche, who was in charge of the greenhouses and gardeners: from Rouen Monet sent tigridias (tiger flowers) and wallflowers, passion flowers for the temperate house and curious little nasturtiums – all except for the perennials destined for the greenhouses. "Tell Eugene it would be wise to cover the tigridias and other things that he knows about, as there might be a frost, especially with the moon. Ask him also, in case of sharp showers or hail (we had some here yesterday), to take down the canvases on the greenhouse': the garden and his painting, his twin *raisons d'être*.

As Monet's income grew, so Alice became once more the attentive hostess she had once been, taking delight in being able to offer hospitality as in the old days. Some of the friends who came had also known her at Rottembourg, such as Carolus-Duran; many others were artists such as Sisley and Renoir. Other visitors included Americans from London and Paris, including Sargent and Whistler, and Americans living at Giverny, such as their son-in-law Thodore Butler, Lilla Cabot Perry, artist and wife of Thomas Perry, great nephew of the celebrated Commodore Perry, Guy and Ethel Rose, and Peggy Hart and his wife. Writers among the guests at Giverny included the exquisite Mallarmé, Paul Valéry, highly amusing contrary to all expectations, Mirbeau, sharp, sensitive and extremely funny, Thadée and Misia Natanson, and the Guitrys, father and son, with Charlotte Lysés and Rodin. Monet also invited the critic Gustave Geffroy so that he could meet Cézanne, who came to Giverny to paint in 1894: "We shall expect you on Wednesday. I hope that Cézanne will still be here and will also come, but he is so singular, so nervous of seeing new faces that I'm afraid he may let us down, despite wishing so much to meet you." The brilliant but capricious Cézanne was evidently difficult to tie down.

Looking through to the kitchen from the dining room. As so often in the house, yellow gives way to blue. On the walls are two prints by Utamaro, Two Masked Actors *and* The Child who played with a Bear and his Mother *often depicted as a Witch.*

View of the garden from the studio-sitting room.

The "Epicerie" or spice store, beneath a Sadahide print depicting the transport of merchandise from Yokohama, 1861.

Late afternoon in Monet's bedroom.

The list of regular guests was a long one, including of course the Durand-Ruel family, who were always welcome, as later were the dealers Josse and Gaston Bernheim. Giverny was virtually a second home to Georges Clemenceau, and to members of the Académie Goncourt such as the cantankerous Lucien Descaves; in return, there was always a place set for Monet at the Friday dinners held by the "Goncourites" at the Café Drouant. He was also a regular at the Impressionists' dinners at the Café Riche on the first Thursday of every month, at the dinners founded by Mirbeau at Les Bons Cosaques, dinners at La Banlieue, and in London later on he was sponsored as a member of the extremely select Beefsteak Club.

The children and younger generation, meanwhile, had the good fortune to enjoy the company of the colony of American artists who flocked to Giverny. They stayed mostly at the Hôtel Baudy, which became a focus for an endless round of delightful distractions, including costume balls, musical evenings and tennis parties. Most of these artists had come with the idea of becoming disciples of Monet, though Monet steadfastly refused to teach them. Although at first he welcomed them gladly, eventually he closed his door to them: he was working. Among them were large numbers of women artists, or *peintresses*, as the villagers called them. For Blanche — who had painted from an early age, and who was the only one who could claim the benefit of Monet's advice as they often worked side by side on the same subjects — this was an opportunity of which she could only have dreamed.

English became virtually the *lingua franca* at Giverny, as this throng of young people threw themselves into their outdoor pursuits — hunting, fishing, boating and picnics — in joyous liberty. The Hoschedé-Monet children were a familiar sight, boys and girls alike in pink sunhats that Monet had bought from a hatter and that were the talk of the village. Michel Monet, covered in engine grease, loved to tinker with mechanics, and even invented vehicles that worked. With Jean-Pierre Hoschedé, he studied botany under the wise if severe tutelage of Abbe Toussaint, the only friend Monet and Alice had made locally. Jean Monet, meanwhile, loved chemistry. Young Lucien Pissarro and the Sisley children, Jeanne and Pierre, would often come to stay. In summer the Hoschedé girls would go boating, with sunhats, parasols and fishing rods; in winter there would be ice-skating and parties on the frozen marshes, with magnificent Chinese lanterns suspended from the trees. And everybody loved it when Sylvain the chauffeur filled the night air with the notes of his hunting horn.

An invitation to lunch at Giverny brought with it the implied acceptance of an unchanging round of rituals: it was as well to be a gourmand, or perhaps a gourmet, and a lover of all things Japanese, in this house where everything was subject to the rhythms of Monet's working life, and where you had to know how to yield gracefully to a rule and discipline that were almost Benedictine. The daily routine was both strict and sacred, and visits of the house and grounds followed carefully ordained routes.

Some visitors came by train, and were met by Gaston the innkeeper in a horse-drawn carriage, or later by Sylvain in the Panhard. Monet was invariably unhappy when people chose to come in their own motor cars, as they frequently suffered several punctures between Paris and Giverny and — the thing that he detested above all else —

arrived late. Gaston's passengers would ring at the little garden door, while hardy motorists would drive through the main gate to alight at the foot of the veranda.

For over half a century, the dining room at Giverny saw guests from many different worlds and virtually every continent. Monet and Alice maintained close links with every prominent Japanese figure in Paris, and with some in Tokyo. And close friends such as Clemenceau would invite themselves to lunch before setting off on their travels:

> *Dear friend,*
>
> *I shall come and bid you farewell on Wednesday, taking advantage of the opportunity to cadge lunch off you. In return, I shall bring you my appetite…*

After lunch, according to the unchanging ritual, guests would retire to the studio-sitting room to take coffee and to look at Monet's paintings, the most recent of which were propped against the walls or placed on easels. Privileged guests were allowed upstairs to view the collection of other artists' works in the private rooms of their host and hostess.

Before entering the dining room, with its wonderful array of prints, visitors might do well, however, to pause for a moment to consider the art of Japan. According to the well-known story, Monet bought his first Japanese prints in Holland in the early 1870s. But he had in fact already been collecting them for many years, though clearly not examples of the finest quality. The prints that according to his

Claude Monet, The House, *1920s, Musée Marmottan-Monet, Paris. Monet painted this view when he was suffering from cataracts.*

own account he found when playing truant in Le Havre, had been brought back from Japan by the great ships en route to German, Dutch, British and American ports with their cargo of oriental foodstuffs and objects of all sorts. So it was that he came across some poor-quality prints on sale among the knickknacks in a little shop in Le Havre. We do not know which of his prints were the first in his collection, moreover. It was his friend Théodore Duret, who accompanied Cernuschi to Japan, who introduced him to large numbers of albums and prints of the finest quality. Despite Japan's self-imposed isolation since 1639, the Dutch East India Company had established a trading post at the port of Nagasaki and other channels by which it was able to transport porcelain and works of art (of variable quality, admittedly) via Batavia (present-day Jakarta). At a time when entry to Japan by foreigners (other than the Dutch at Nagasaki) and export of any Japanese goods was illegal under penalty of death, this represented a real tour de force on the part of this nation of intrepid merchants and mariners. All this was of course to change with Commodore Matthew Perry's armed expedition of 1853.

Japanese tea houses and galleries of Japanese art now opened in western cities, to become literary salons frequented by the intelligentsia. Japanese art dealers opened businesses in Paris, such as Matsukaba who introduced Vever and Monet, and Mme Desoye's shop La Porte Chinoise on rue de Rivoli. Japanese art and artefacts attracted an eager clientele including Degas, Carolus-Duran, the publisher Charpentier, Fantin-Latour and Zola, as well as Monet. Siegfried Bing, who introduced Monet to Edmond de Goncourt in 1892, founded the illustrated review *Le Japon Artistique*.

The west garden beneath the clematis arches, showing iris, sweet rocket and Clematis "Nelly Moser" to the right.

Monet was not only an astute collector but also a generous one, for if he was constantly buying Japanese prints by the hundred, he also gave many of them away. "Do you like Japanese prints? Do choose one," were phrases frequently heard at Giverny during the time of Monet and Alice as well as in later generations. Monet's collection reflected his passions for nature, the theatre (to which he often went) and music (he was a devotee of the famous Concerts Pasdeloup). Above all, it was the collection of an aesthete who loved the rural life, botany and entomology. The scenes of daily life depicted in the art of *ukiyo-e* ("visions of the floating world") found echoes in the favourite themes of some of the Impressionist painters. Prints that poked fun at European ways, meanwhile, recalled scenes painted on folding screens by Japanese artists of the late sixteenth and early seventeenth centuries. These lampooned European missionaries and merchants – before their expulsion from Japan as the country isolated itself from the outside world – in a style of art known as *namban byobu*, meaning literally "southern barbarians': in other words Europeans.

Paintings and prints covered the walls in all the rooms at Giverny, including Monet's studio sitting room. Whatever their motifs, themes or subjects, the Japanese prints drew the viewer into a world that was "other". With their skilful use of polychrome they captured a world in movement, where all is gesture (courtesans with their kamuro, the stylized movements of Kabuki actors), rhythm and cadence. Even the landscapes, both small and large in scale, depicted a life of intensity and motion, the antithesis of stasis.

The dining room was enlarged to incorporate the original kitchen, so becoming a large, light-filled rectangular space with two sets of french windows opening on to the veranda. The floor tiles from Saint-Just, in a white and deep red chequerboard pattern that is very popular in the region, complements the two tones of chrome yellow on the ceiling, walls and furniture: the tall mantelpiece with its blue tiles framing the fireplace, where you expect to see a brass chafing dish to keep the dishes warm; the table, designed for twelve but able to accommodate sixteen; the sheaf back chairs; the sideboards and wainscoting; and above all the pair of Cauchois cabinets with their displays of blue faience from Rouen and Delft, Chinese and Japanese porcelain, a splendid blue and white "rice-grain" soup tureen, and a pink East India Company centrepiece from Rottembourg. The graceful vase on the mantelpiece with its bat motif was a gift from the great enthusiast for all things Japanese Raymond Koechlin, and is flanked by some very simple green Vallauris pottery.

The mantelpiece wall is covered with prints, densely and elegantly hung by Monet in an arrangement that reveals a Hiroshiga who is not just a landscape artist and lampoonist of Europeans (as the visitor will see him in the blue sitting room), but also an astonishing artist of the natural world, both in his cranes from the flowers and birds series and in the fish series that hangs on another of the walls. This room also boasts a beautiful set of Utamaro portraits of women, both Japanese – courtesans of the "green houses" of which he compiled a virtual directory – and European.

The kitchen, showing the faïence tiles from Rouen, made using rare cobalt blue, and the fireplace with its roasting spit.

The Kitchen

In a home and family where food played such an important part, the kitchen was sacrosanct. In Monet's time, the notion of showing the kitchen to visitors would have seemed outlandish: at this period the kitchen was the unchallenged dominion of the cook and her kitchen maids, where the other servants came to eat their meals. In this utilitarian space *par excellence*, any aesthetic considerations were – in most households – an optional extra.

Not here, however. The polished red floor tiles are from the renowned tile-works of Saint-Just in the Beauvais region, the wall tiles, with their patterns in cobalt blue (rare because expensive to produce) from Rouen. Even the fireplace with its roasting spit is tiled, and all this blue serves to highlights the warmth of the impressive and immaculately polished copper *batterie de cuisine*. The walls, ceiling, furniture, table, stools, ice box and salt box are all painted blue – a colour recommended to young housewives-to-be for its hygienic properties, as it was supposed to repel insects, especially flies.

Monet, who never set foot in the kitchen, must have done so for the first and last time when he chose this shade of blue: a pale royal blue highlighted with coeruleum blue, which he was to use widely throughout the house. This combination of blues was then varnished to provide even more light in a room which had two windows as well as french windows opening straight on to the veranda, and which – like the rest of the rooms in the house – overlooked the garden.

The arrangement of the kitchen reflects the functional requirements of the time: a small window opening on to the street was where the vegetable gardener tapped every day to announce the arrival of the previous day's order of vegetables, fruit and salad, all grown in the large terraced vegetable garden of the Maison Bleue at the other end of the village. Steps beside this window led down to the cellar, where perishable items could be put away in the cool atmosphere without delay. Blocks of ice for the ice box came from Vernon.

The presiding deity of the kitchen, however, was the enormous stove fuelled by wood and coal, with its hot water tank under a copper lid and its two stoves. Very early every morning, this had to be coaxed into life and stoked up to provide enough heat to cook breakfast to suit everyone's individual tastes (for Monet alone this meant grilled *andouillette* sausages, bacon and all manner of other peculiar habits picked up on his travels), lunches of Rabelaisian generosity and scale, not to speak of scones, muffins and pastries for tea, followed by dinner. Everyday family meals would be for ten plus the servants, swelling to considerably more when there were guests (who were only ever invited to lunch).

Like every other house of substance, Giverny was ruled by a succession – and sometimes dynasties – of cooks. Some, like Caroline and Mélanie, have bequeathed recipes in their names. Of all the cooks who reigned over this kitchen, the last and probably the best was Marguerite, who came to work at the house as a girl, introduced her fiancé Paul to Monet (who promptly offered him a job so as to be sure of keeping Marguerite), and presided over the great stove until 1939.

The kitchen was a constant hive of activity, leaving little time to relax: once the chopping, cooking and washing up were done, there were the serried ranks of copper saucepans, fish kettles, bains-marie and pots and pans of every description to be scoured, polished and covered with tulle – until the next time, which was never very long.

In rare moments of repose, Marguerite would sit in a little low armless chair from Lorraine and leaf through the venerable *Pot-au-feu* recipe book for inspiration – or simply gaze at the delicate pink and white blossom of the two crab apple trees outside the windows. After her return to her native Berry, she recalled: "The work was hard at Giverny, but as I cooked I had before me my two Japanese crab apples [*Malus floribunda*]."

Batterie de cuisine for a food-loving family. The large cooker with its hot water tank.

In this room which is an art gallery in itself, family and visitors – including distinguished Japanese visitors such as the Kurokis and Monsieur Hayashi – would eat beneath the gaze of this exotic cast of characters at a table laid with a cloth dyed by Delphine the linen maid and set with a blue Creil faience ware Japan service known as the "cherry tree", or a white porcelain service with a broad yellow border edged with a blue fillet. The curtains, in organdie also dyed yellow, are drawn back to let in the light. Two tall narrow mirrors face each other, one with a flower holder in blue Rouen faience, the other with a grey and blue Japanese flower holder in the form of a fan, beneath which stands a large Ming vase.

After lunch, family and guests retired to the studio-sitting room – which took three years to transform into a decent, comfortable studio. The barn with its beaten earth floor was linked to the house by an internal staircase and opensed into the Epicerie. Above the porte-cochère, which has been preserved, a fanlight allowed more light to filter in.

Pitch pine, a wood then very much in vogue, was used in every room, for stairs, floors and wainscoting, and even for the studio furniture, including a small cabinet glazed above and with a set of drawers below, a large table with a deep drawer for sketches, drawings, pastels and the like, and picture crates.

Light floods into the studio through a south-facing window and above all a vast west-facing bay window. The more usual arrangement by which studios are lit by large north-facing windows was impossible here because of the presence of the first floor. This large west window indicates that Monet did not intend to linger too long there, and that one day he knew he would have a "proper" studio.

But for the moment this was his studio, which became a sitting room when he wasn't working: hence the two desks, one for Alice and the other for Monet (both wrote prolifically and every day) and the Cuban mahogany secretaire under the large window, for filing papers. Rattan chairs, cane tables, a music table, a chest with a Renaissance front piled high with books, chintz-covered easy chairs, their arms cluttered with shawls, pretty rattan armchairs and capacious sofas, once covered with calico printed with a stylized mango design. Arranged on the plate rail above the wainscoting are a pair of fine Japanese earthenware pieces, two Chinese vases, some early blue Japanese for export by the British or Dutch East India Company, brush pots hollowed out of enormous bamboo stems, tea boxes and the like.

Very large flower arrangements of a single species and flower were dotted throughout the room, while small blown-glass bowls served as bud vases. Persian rugs laid on the polished boards added a note of elegance to the room. You can picture Monet sitting at his desk, scratching away with his quill pen on his pale grey headed notepaper in his long battle to gain entry into the Louvre collections for Manet's *Olympia*. At the instigation of his friend John Singer Sargent, he devoted a year to sending begging letters to his friends in order to raise a subscription of 200,000 francs, so that he could present the painting to the museum.

This was a room for work followed by conversation, where with Alice he received family and friends, as well as dealers, collectors and fellow artists. It was also the

The chrome yellow dining room, where meals were served on a Creil Japan ware service called Au cerisier *("Cherry Tree").*

setting for the wedding breakfast after the marriage of Suzanne – Monet's favourite model, whom he depicted in the two version of *Woman with a Parasol* now in the Louvre – to the American painter Theodore Butler. This was also where guests enjoyed coffee after lunch, with a glass of home-made fruit brandy or other *digestif*. All around, every inch of wall space was densely hung with paintings, arranged as many as four deep from the wainscoting to the ceiling, the hanging scheme varying according to sales, as well as Monet's mood and recent travels. Thus the studio-sitting room might whisk visitors off to Belle-Ile, the Creuse and frequently the Normandy coastline, or further afield to everywhere from Bordighera to London and from Norway to Venice.

Comfortable as the room was, it was never – for lack of that north-facing window – a very good studio. But it did provide a working space for Monet to accomplish the feat of completing his Mediterranean paintings, from Bordighera to Antibes, a reminder of his prodigious *"mémoire en atelier"*. This page of history covering over forty years of his working life reveals every stage on a journey tormented by doubt and extreme mental suffering, of which his correspondence reveals the frequency and depth. Yet the proportions and above all the size of the paintings hung here so densely recall the words of Sacha Guitry: "Claude Monet seems to have cut his paintings out of canvases measuring at least 30 square metres. He may enclose them in frames, but we are well aware that the sky does not end there."

With the construction of the second studio at the end of the century, the studio-sitting room became simply a sitting room, where Monet kept the paintings with which he could not bear to part, and even some that he had sold and then bought back again. His emotional links with his paintings always remained strong. Once sold, his poor paintings were confined within hanging schemes, bought again, sold again, swapped, forgotten in dreary museums where as often as not they were hidden behind doors, or simply ignored. A laughing stock to the ignorant, easy prey to snobs, even raised to absurd heights to influential enthusiasts, they would be much better off in a family home.

A few of the paintings in the sitting room could pen their own memoirs of their trials and tribulations. During their difficult years at Vétheuil, for instance, Monet offered to sell *Vétheuil in the Fog*, painted in 1879, to the baritone Jean-Baptiste Faure for fifty francs. Faure decided that it was too white, the paint was too thin, and it was impossible anyway to tell what it was meant to be. On a visit to Giverny many years later, Faure saw the painting in the studio-sitting room and expressed his interest. Monet retorted that it was no longer for sale, no matter how high the price, and reminded Faure of the circumstances in which he had seen the painting before. Faure, wrong-footed, made his excuses and left.

Altogether more upsetting was the chequered career of *Women in the Garden*, the refusal of which by the Salon of 1867 left Monet distraught and penniless. Coming to the aid of his friend, Frédéric Bazille bought the painting for 2,500 francs, in five monthly payments, and sent it to his parents' house in the Midi. After Bazille, who was godfather to Jean Monet, was killed in action at Beaune-la-Rolande during the Franco-Prussian War, his parents wanted to buy a faithful portrait of their son by

Renoir from its then owner, Edouard Manet. Manet was unwilling to sell them the portrait, doubtless because he felt it was bad form, but agreed to exchange it for Monet's *Women in the Garden*. Monet, who was deeply attached to this composition that he had painted at Ville-d'Avray, agreed with Manet to swap it for a portrait by Manet of Camille in the garden at Argenteuil. For reasons that may never be fully understood, since he was distressed to see it go and by that time was far from poor, in 1921 Monet decided to part with the painting, and sold it to the French state for 200,000 francs. The painting entered the collections of the Musée de Luxembourg, moving to the Louvre only in 1934.

The *Turkeys* that Monet painted for the rotunda drawing room at Rottembourg in 1876, meanwhile, was passed from Hoschedé to Giuseppe De Nittis, Duret and finally Depeaux, staying within this circle of close friends. On 28 February 1903, Monet wrote to Durand-Ruel from Giverny:

> *For my part I would be happy to see the Turkeys canvas again, so in short I have accepted Monsieur Depeaux's offer to exchange it for two paintings of his choice, with the exception of the London and Garden series. I'm not in the habit of going back on my promises, and to be blunt do not want to be the turkey in this story…*

But the tale of the *Turkeys* was soon to have a happy ending: in 1906 Depeaux sold the painting to Prince Edmond de Polignac, and on her death in 1943 the Princesse de Polignac (*née* Singer) bequeathed it to the Louvre.

An attentive host, Monet enjoyed showing his guests his recent acquisitions. Immediately above the studio-sitting room lay his bedroom, lit by three large windows, two south-facing and one west-facing, and simply decorated with white walls hung with damask panels sewn edge to edge. It was furnished with a

The blue sitting room, known at different periods as the salon bleu or the salon mauve: a room for sitting and chatting, with in its cabinet a handsome edition of Van Houtte's Flora, often consulted by Monet.

The Japanese Prints

Traditional Japanese prints are printed from wood, with the motifs engraved into blocks of catalpa or cherry wood. Their characteristic images of the ephemeral and evanescent, of the fleeting moment, filled with joy or pain, became known in Japan as *ukiyo-e*, meaning "images of the floating world". The distant descendant of Buddhist art and of the Tosa and Kano schools of painting, the genre encapsulated a highly specific world, and reached its heyday between the mid-eighteenth and the mid-nineteenth century. This exotic, unfamiliar universe was introduced to France by Edmond de Goncourt, Isaac de Camondo, Henri Vever, Charles Baudelaire and Philippe Burty among others, not forgetting the productive and enlightening expeditions of Théodore Duret and Henri Cernuschi, whose glorious collections can still be admired in Paris today.

For centuries Japanese art was divided, perhaps even torn, between depictions of purely Japanese scenes and others that acknowledged the influence of China. At a time of political upheaval, with successive changes in the ruling classes, artistic tastes came to be flaunted more openly. It is interesting to note in this context that *ukiyo-e* prints were an immediate success with both men of cultivated tastes, who were prepared to pay high prices for them, and with the more popular classes.

While clearly showing the influences of the schools of earlier centuries, such as the Tosa and Kano, artists of the *ukiyo-e* school owed their unique talent and power to their virtuoso skill in applying traditional and classic techniques to images of the contemporary world. By the mid-nineteenth century, eastern and western artists alike had grown weary of depicting elaborate pilgrimages, religious feast days, heroic military victories, the noble feats of great lords, life at court and scenes from myth and legend. But the intellectual upheavals that shook both eastern and western civilizations at different periods nevertheless preserved a shared passion for studies of nature, as seen in the fine Japanese tradition of making trips to admire the cherry trees in blossom, or in scenes of glowing red maples or of daily life.

With their peerless skill in polychrome printing, the multi-talented Japanese printmakers of the floating world, this real world of nuances so subtle that they were barely palpable, moved effortlessly from scenes of striking simplicity to grotesque characters; from explicit eroticism to landscapes; from tender images of motherhood to elegant depictions of ladies of fashion, and especially the highly cultivated geishas of the Green Houses; from exquisitely detailed renderings of subjects from natural history to kabuki theatre actors; and from the comical posturings of western merchants at trading posts to the imperious splendour of the great merchant ships under their cosmopolitan flags.

If the relatively crude images of the *otsu-e* school of Japanese folk painting became well known and appealed particularly to the tourist market, a seventeenth-century source claimed unequivocally that only the art of *ukiye-o*, and "neither the Kano nor the Tosa school", could "depict the great adventure of the Yoshiwara" (the closed quarter containing the Green Houses). Although many of the scenes it depicted, which appealed to all social classes, could be described as popular or even vulgar, the prodigious expertise in traditional techniques displayed by its greatest artists combined with the innate judgement and refinement of the Japanese, saved even the most trivial scene from descending into vulgarity. While Commodore Robert Perry's landmark expeditions to Japan in 1852-4 may have sounded the death knell for the civilization of old Japan, they allowed the refinement and genius of Japanese culture to flourish with as much vitality as ever

Left:

*Hiroshige (1797-1858),
The Naruto Whirlpools at
Awa, from his Famous Views
of the Sixty-odd Provinces,
Fondation Claude Monet,
Giverny.*

*Hokusai (1760-1849),
The Great Wave off
Kanagawa, from the
Thirty-six views of Mount Fuji,
Fondation Claude Monet,
Giverny.*

Ci-cons:

*Hiroshige, Asakusa Rice
Fields during the Festival
of the Cock, from One
Hundred Famous Views
of Edo: a catponders the
festival of the cock before
the arrival of the new year.
Fondation Claude Monet,
Giverny.*

Louis XVI secretaire, two commodes, and a bed, bonnetière and nest of tables all painted in pale yellow. But the luxury of this room lay in its collection of paintings, which spilled over into Alice's room and the two bathrooms: a treasure store including three works by Delacroix, twelve by Cézanne (including *The Negro Scipio* hanging over Monet's bathtub), nine by Renoir, five by Berthe Morisot (including *The Bath, The Bowl of Milk, Girl with Greyhound* and *West Cowes*), and a Corot. Then came two Caillebottes, three Pissarros, four Jongkinds, his portrait by Déodat de Séverac, a Sisley, a Degas, a Fantin-Latour and a seascape by Marquet. In addition to the oils there were pastels by Morisot, Manet and Vuillard, water-colours by Chéret, Signac (two), Jongkind (several) and Sargent, and a pair of Rodin sculptures.

A visit to this little private gallery would be followed by a walk in the garden, a visit to the greenhouses, and a cup of tea in the blue sitting room, known at different times as the Salon Mauve or the Salon Bleu, where (as Julie Manet noted) even the wainscoting was painted blue. With its end wall occupied entirely by a pattern of doors, its French eighteenth-century feel, and its blue to which Monet added his own special alchemy – two classic shades of blue as revisited by an Impressionist painter – this room has its own special charm. Furniture painted in these two shades of blue includes the cabinet that holds a handsome edition of Louis van Houtte's *Flora*, beside a chintz sofa, rattan chairs, cane marquetry tables and some charming English officers' tables, and an upright piano. Crowds of guests would squeeze into this small, intimate room, while Monet carried on working in his studio, meditating in his bedroom, or contending with the fading light or fickle weather as he worked outside.

The previous owners of Giverny sadly replaced this room's original terracotta tiles – with their lovely proportions and warm tones brought out by beeswax polish – with patterned tiles, for a more "modern" look. This was the room where the

Yoshifuji (1828-87), American Amusements, 1861. Fondation Claude Monet, Giverny.

Utamaro (1753-1806), page from an album published at Edo in 1791, Competition of Poetry on the One Thousand One Hundred Birds. Fondation Claude Monet, Giverny.

Hiroshige, The Torch Shrine in Oki Province, *from the* Famous Views of the Sixty-odd Provinces. *Fondation Claude Monet, Giverny.*

post was opened, where people chatted and made tea – which they might drink anywhere according to the weather – with water from the large samovar.

The cocooned atmosphere of the blue sitting room could also be as noisy and full of life and colour as a tropical aviary. Alice would listen to the chatter or read, perhaps closing her eyes sometimes and allowing her thoughts to wander back to another drawing room long ago. If she had any regrets she was careful not to show them, however, and the sensitive and artistic sides of her character could hardly have been more fulfilled. When Monet was away, he often wrote to say how much he was looking forward to unpacking his new paintings in the studio and looking at them with her. If there was one constant in her life, it was the company of paintings. The simple elegance of this room, hung by Monet with most of his collection of Hiroshige prints, must surely have delighted her. The colours chosen by Monet to decorate the house – a classic palette revisited by his own artist's eye – have something curiously astringent about them, nuances of citrus tones, charged with energy: from the blue of the kitchen to the yellow of the dining room and the other lovely blues of the blue sitting room, these are colours that are dynamic rather than serene. And paradoxically, these bold tones seem to withhold their strength beside the colours of the prints, so that Hiroshige's blues are revealed in all their deep serenity, notably in the *Naruto Whirlpools*, *Monkey Bridge* and *Kajukuri Coast*, dominated by expanses of water. A similar effect may be observed with the pale green Monet used in other rooms and passages, which complements his collection of *aizur-e* prints using exclusively blue pigments. Kuniyoshi's triptych of elegant ladies dressed in blue is inescapably reminiscent of Monet's *Women in the Garden*.

The humorous side of Hiroshige is also revealed here in his satirical *English Delegation at Yokohama*, in which he pokes fun at the military parade, pompous buildings and "Japanese" gardens laid out *à l'anglaise*. Throughout the house, with

Hokusai, Fine Weather with a South Wind, *from the* Thirty-Six Views of Mount Fuji. *Fondation Claude Monet, Giverny.*

the exception of the dining room, Monet would change the hanging schemes according to his mood, perhaps flanking his Hiroshige prints symmetrically with his peerless Hokusai prints of a blue *Mount Fuji* and foaming blue and white *Great Wave*. As he decided on the arrangement and spacing of his prints, it must surely have occurred to him that Hiroshige was almost the exact contemporary (within a year; Hokusai was a little earlier) of another occupant of the house, Delacroix. This room was a cosy refuge, in front of a roaring fire, in wild weather, when the rains of Normandy could recall another Hiroshige print depicting *Oshashi Bridge and Atake in a Sudden Shower.*

Monet had arrived at Giverny in 1883, yet as the century drew to a close he still did not have a proper studio: it was high time to build one now. Beside the west gate to the garden lay a small plot that – in the convoluted way of rural France, with its complicated network of boundary markers, enclaves and parcels squeezed between ancient walls – was still the property of the previous owner and had been leased to Monet. Now at last he bought this tumbledown building and demolished it, keeping only its aviary, which was to become a sanctuary for wounded birds. On the site he built a second studio, the studio of which he had always dreamed, carefully designed to provide everything he needed in the way of space and light, with an immense north-facing window and even a large section of glazing in the roof.

Pale winter sunlight.

The studio-sitting room, where family and visitors would enjoy coffee and perhaps a glass of home-made plum brandy, in the company of the little Venus slipper orchid and the paintings from which Monet refused to be parted – all watched over by a bust of the artist by Paulin.

Detail of bamboo furniture in the "Epicerie", a vogue launched by the great universal exhibitions of the Victorian era.

A staircase, its walls lined with prints, led up to this large square space, which opened on to a long open gallery overlooking the greenhouses. The furniture included a mahogany desk for Monet's prolific writings and a pitch pine glass-fronted armoire holding stacks of papers, with beautiful Japanese objects — oiled paper parasols, wooden houses and the like — scattered all around. Cabinets held Monet's Baedekers for his travels, English plant catalogues and a host of other books. There were sofas to accommodate visiting collectors and dealers, and a rocking chair belonging to Anna, Jacques Hoschedé's Norwegian daughter-in-law (the mezzanine floor had apartments for Jacques Hoschedé and his wife Inga, and for Jean Monet and his wife Blanche Hoschedé). This was Monet's private world, where he could work in cloistered peace and quiet.

A third studio, known as the Large Water Lily Studio, was built over the ruins of another dilapidated building on the extreme eastern edge of the grounds. Started at the outbreak of the First World War and completed in astonishing time in 1915, despite the general mobilization, this studio was to be of vast proportions, measuring 15 metres tall, 23 metres long and 12 metres wide, with a detachable awning to filter the light at will. Designed to accommodate the vast panels that would one day hang in the Orangerie in the Tuileries gardens, this building horrified Monet with its ugliness. Soon it was duly covered in ivy. And so this artist of the outdoors acquired his third studio.

Monet's bedroom, where he kept his collection of paintings by friends and works by older masters who had fallen from fashion, such as Corot and Delacroix.

The Clos Normand

Leaning on the balustrade of the veranda and taking in the view of the garden down to the Chemin du Roy, it is impossible not to smile at the understatement of Monet's letter to Durand-Ruel in early June 1883: "then the garden has absorbed some of my time, so that I can pick a few flowers to paint when the weather is bad…"

In fact, from his arrival at Giverny that year to the end of his life, he was to oversee the sowing of thousands of seeds, the planting of hundreds of plant species, and the unloading of countless railway wagon-loads of topsoil to improve the unproductive Giverny soil. By the end of the first summer he had won his race against time, and was able to pick poppies, mallows, chrysanthemums, sunflowers, dahlias, white and yellow marguerites, gladioli, cobaea, scarlet and Japanese lilies and – in due course and in a sheltered spot – the first Christmas roses. More than enough to create generous arrangements for his Chinese vases and to inspire eighteen panels of various sizes for the doors of the large drawing room of the Durand-Ruel residence in rue de Rome.

Regardless of the precarious nature of his financial position, Monet was already in thrall to his horticultural passion, and lost no time in lavishing large sums on the

Left:
The former orchard, now the west garden. The fruit trees were replaced with ornamental cherries and crab apples, standing in beds edged with aubrietia.

Right:
Standard roses, peonies and iris.

The central path in autumn, invaded by nasturtiums.

garden. As at Argenteuil, his friendship with Caillebotte was to play an essential part in this adventure, even though – great painter, outstanding botanist and skilled gardener though he was – Caillebotte never created so personal a garden for himself, and certainly not a painter's garden. Giverny also inspired the enthusiasm of others of Monet's friends who were also good gardeners, including Mallarmé, for whom life without flowers was unthinkable, Clemenceau, Mirbeau and even Guitry.

Five years later, Monet painted *Young Girl in the Garden at Giverny*, a painting that speaks volumes for the task he had accomplished by then: a young girl, Maine, is shown walking up the central path, her arms filled with flowers, amid flowerbeds of dense luxuriance and finely judged balance. The Clos Normand, so named by Georges Truffaut, heralded the true *fin-de-siècle* apotheosis of the simplicity and splendour that was to continue to grow and flourish until the 1930s.

That Monet was a born painter was never in doubt, but where did this passion for gardening – and this rare talent for it – come from?

For this young Parisian growing up in the provinces there were no walks in the Bois de Boulogne, no playing in sand pits under the trees of Parisian squares, no getting lost in the maze in the Jardin des Plantes or sailing toy boats in the fountains of the Luxembourg or Tuileries gardens. What there was, by contrast, was a charming garden looking out over the sea at Sainte-Adresse, near Le Havre where he grew up. Three motifs seduced him there: *Jeanne-Marguerite Lecadre in the Garden*, showing his cousin strolling in the garden, dressed in white beneath a white parasol; *Flowering Garden at Sainte-Adresse*; and *Garden at Saint-Adresse*, depicting his young cousin again, this time standing by the greenery-festooned balustrade talking to a male friend, while his aunt Lecadre and his father watch a regatta from the terrace. Though strongly influenced by contemporary taste, Sainte-Adresse – with its dense planting and sense of luxuriant freedom – was no ordinary garden.

Then came the startlingly modern *Women in the Garden*, painted at Ville-d'Avray at the same period, an ode to the grace of female figures in an outdoor setting which heralded Monet's lifelong infatuation with capturing the fleeting play of sunlight and shade on posies and dresses, ravishing here in their whirl of movement.

We know that Monet started gardening at Argenteuil, but this still gives little clue as to the true sources of the deep-seated inspiration that make the gardens at Giverny so original. When he was painting for the Hoschedés at the Château de Rottembourg, he ignored the formal parterres beside the house with their Medici urns in favour of the wilder and more natural landscapes of the park, with their irresistible white turkeys and unruly rambling roses beside the lake. In Holland, he did paintings of the tulip fields which are in fact extraordinary outsize beds of blooms in brilliant colours juxtaposed in immensities of flat space; in Paris, he painted the Jardin de l'Infante from the Louvre colonnade, and not until ten years later the Tuileries gardens and Parc Monceau; in London, Hyde Park and Green Park. And therein lay the surprise for him, surely: in the discovery of these Victorian and Edwardian gardens in the heart of a city that was one itself one large garden.

In the letters that Monet sent home from his travels, the only garden of which he spoke with true enthusiasm was the Moreno Garden at Bodighera, less a garden

Espalier fruit trees near the Water Lily Studio.

Autumn arrives with dahlias, asters and all the yellows of the sunflower family.

than a vast and extraordinary park, dense, exuberant and teeming with rare and exotic Mediterranean species that he had never seen before, and that fascinated him. "Monet the taciturn," as his friend Thadée Natanson dubbed him, who so often seemed reluctant to express himself in writing, penned long, eloquent and profusely detailed letters about the magical gardens at Bodighera. Writing to Alice in February 1884, when everyone at Giverny was complaining of the bitter cold, he could barely contain his rapturous admiration: "a delightful walk, discovering every hidden corner of this incomparable garden... a garden such as this defies description, it is simply magical, with every plant in the world growing freely and apparently untended, a careless confusion of every type of palm, every variety of orange and mandarin tree..." Going on to eulogize over the olive trees, the particular blue of the sky, the pink colour of everything that he had never seen elsewhere, he worried that he would never be able to capture all this: "Everything I do is flame de punch or dapple grey [*gorge-de-pigeon*]... and what a pretty garden that will make. The prevailing colour here is an extraordinary, inexpressible pink..."

Curiously, there is no record of any mention by Monet of the pavilions and hothouses of the Universal Exhibitions held in Paris in 1867, 1878 and 1889 – and yet we know he visited them. The eagerly awaited Japanese display at the 1867 exhibition included a horticultural section occupying a quarter of the area of the Champ de Mars, with hothouses revealing to western eyes the magic of orchids. Monet wrote not a word about this, however, nor about the exhibitions of 1878 or even 1889 (when preparations for the Clos Normand were in full swing), which included a display featuring the flora of the French colonies, with a plethora of spectacular exhibits from the botanical gardens in Saigon and the Ile Bourbon (Réunion). True, he did not appear to be unduly impressed either by the appearance that same year of the Eiffel Tower, soaring high into the Paris sky and difficult to ignore. Doubtless at these highly international events this paradoxical and enigmatic figure – who left behind him neither diaries nor plans for his garden – had eyes only for the Japanese displays.

Monet grasped the potential of the Clos Normand – space that had been buried beneath a garden that was at once distressingly mediocre in its planting and suffocatingly pompous in its conception – immediately. Already he was conceiving his garden here in the same way that he conceived his paintings, and the same principles that were to govern the Clos Normand would be applied a little later to the water garden. Nothing was to be planted without the most careful thought. Monet was intending to plant to paint, not to paint what was planted – the two were inseparable, needless to say, but in making this garden Monet was also creating the subjects of his paintings.

The balance of the whole flower garden rested on the central avenue, its spinal column. Henceforth everything would be designed around the precious slope flanking the main path. The spirit of the garden was tangible. Wherever you stood, you had to be able to see the whole planted area. The lime trees beside the second studio, on the west side of the garden, were pollarded to reveal the view to the hill that is so invaluable for predicting the weather: a dense mist, grey and still, means rain or overcast skies; an outline of bluish mist, delicate and moving, means sunshine.

The structure of the Clos Normand demonstrates the importance to Monet of geometrical forms: oblong and round beds in front of the house; rectangles

*The view from Monet's bedroom clearly reveals the structure of the garden.
Lying on axis with the central path are the water lily pond and its great weeping willow.*

broken up by metal verticals on the east side; squares set in the lawn on the west. And articulating the whole space are the major axes and diagonals.

It is a strangely cool framework to underpin a landscape of such warmth: skilfully concealed beneath this artfully tousled scene, apparently imbued with perfect liberty, is an unexpected and skilfully concealed conventionality. Monet's first point of attack was the trees that had clearly been the pride of the former owners: he spared the pair of yews marking the entrance to the central path, but felled the cypresses and abolished the drearily mundane box-edged beds. The Norway spruce, following lengthy and delicate negotiations with Alice, who hated to see a tree felled, were nominally spared. Ruthlessly pruned, reduced to half their height and turned into supports for roses to climb up, the mutilated stumps gradually gave up the unequal struggle, rotted and died. Monet could breathe at last – and so could the path. Great rose-covered arches created a tunnel of greenery open to the light and sun. Beneath them, flower beds ran the length of the path on both sides, becoming broad slightly sloping cushions, regular and slightly conical in shape, offering a double east-west axis as well as a gradual incline from the taller flowers behind to the nasturtiums that festooned themselves over the semi-fine sand, itself raked as in a Japanese garden, so that the ground itself is patterned.

A winter view through the fruit trees of the east garden to the second studio, its gallery overlooking the greenhouses still open.

But – captivating though the controlled verve and lushness of the central path and its constant flowers may be – there is more to draw the eye. The broad beds arranged parallel to it now claim the visitor's attention. Once the great expanse of mauve *Iris pallida* has finished flowering, for example, the eye is drawn systematically on,

The east garden, beside the Water Lily Studio with its espaliered fruit trees. This part of the garden is filled with bulbs, with drifts of autumn crocuses in particular.

beyond its foliage, to the next parallel bed. Everything is subtly and continuously in movement. Along the length of the Chemin du Roy, the wall was lowered to allow uninterrupted views from the house, stretching far beyond to the landscape of undulating fields of cereal crops and wild flowers, as far as the sinuous lines of the willows and poplars fringing the Ru – the future water garden. Iron supports attached to the low wall were soon smothered in climbing roses and scarlet nasturtiums, cousins of the classic Victorian "Empress of India".

After the park at Rottembourg and the gentle, flower-filled gardens of the houses at Argenteuil and Vétheuil, the older children were at first taken aback by the sad expanses at Giverny, but were swiftly appointed by Monet as the gardeners who would help to accomplish the first steps towards its "renaissance". Working at Monet's side, whether on the hillsides or beside the water, was a genuine and joyous adventure of exhilarating freedom for budding botanists full of untamed energy. The children set to with a will, collecting the snails that devoured the irises and picking plums and cherries and selling basketfuls of them to travelling fruit sellers to earn a bit of pocket money. With their help and that of a handful of unskilled day labourers, the metamorphosis was soon taking shape before their very eyes.

Before long the orchard had become a garden; the planted area had increased hugely; new plants had been introduced in great numbers and variety, requiring (as Jean-Pierre recalled) very different methods of cultivation; and the greenhouses had developed to the point where they needed specialist care: all this required the skills of a proper head gardener. Doctor Mirbeau, father of the writer

Spring in the west garden.

and himself the happy owner of a garden of great beauty at Rémalard in the Orne region of Normandy, recommended his own gardener's son, Félix Breuil. Two head gardeners were to reign over the Clos Normand and the water lily pond: first of all Félix Breuil, and many years later Lebret, who after Monet's death would continue to work with Blanche and Michel. These two men would successively give their all and repeatedly achieve the impossible under the iron rule of Monet – the true head gardener, firm but fair. Under them worked five qualified assistant gardeners, one of whom was responsible solely for the upkeep of the water lily pond.

Breuil and Lebret always made it a point of pride to keep up to date with the latest horticultural developments, and would talk expertly of cultivation techniques, soil make-up and exposure. Monet would then respond with considerations of aesthetics, cadence and rhythm, but always from the respectful point of view of someone who understood the worth of his workers and knew how to listen to them. Together they worked in true symbiosis to create marvels. Once you crossed the threshold into this world apart, this refuge from that other world outside the walls, in which the days unfolded at the immemorial pace of rural life, time seemed temporarily to stop, and the pace of life slowed in this unmistakably special place.

A few steps bring you to the house, its façade vanishing beneath festoons of Virginia creeper and climbing roses. Climbing plants are given every encouragement to clamber upwards at will: a gap has been left between the wall and the broad wooden boards of the veranda, while a metal framework attached to the veranda allows prolific climbers – such as Monet's favourite rose, "Mermaid",

Rosa *"Madame Alfred Carrière"*.

Standard roses in front of the house, by the lime trees.

which reached up to his bedroom window – to scramble up to five or six metres. Here and there the climbers on the house and on the veranda intertwine, forming a tunnel of flowers and foliage along the front of the house. At the foot of the front steps, round and oval flowerbeds edged with closely pruned grey foliage overflow with pelargoniums in two shades of pink ochre, echoing the pink of the façade. Further off, near the limes, more oval beds hold taller plantings of standard roses and swirling cobaea, edged with the carefully shaped grey foliage of pinks, with occasional splashes of oenothera (evening primrose), in touches reminiscent of Sainte-Adresse, Argenteuil and above all Caillebotte's garden at Yerres. Did Monet, so private in his innermost thoughts, sometimes yield to the impulse to re-create moments from his past?

The orchard was now in a way the "west garden", an immaculate sweep of lawn with a handful of the old fruit trees serving as supports for vigorous climbing roses such as "Belle Vichysoisse" and "Paul's Himalayan Musk", while others were replaced by apple and Japanese crab apple trees (*Malus floribunda*). Elegantly arranged in the lawn was a sequence of large square beds filled with oriental poppies massed in a single shade – red, white or pink – bordered with iris, or simply with expanses of iris, also of a single colour. Gradually all the beds would be bordered with every species of the iris family that was one of Monet's great passions.

In the "east garden", meanwhile, pergolas were smothered with a ravishing array of clematis: pink and white *C. montana*, deep purple "Jackmanii", delicate pink "Nelly Moser" and the very old *C. japonica* and *C. rehderiana*, with their pretty bell-shaped

Monet could breathe at last – and so could the path. Great rose-covered arches created a tunnel of greenery open to the light and sun. Beneath them, flower beds ran the length of the path on both sides, becoming broad slightly sloping cushions, regular and slightly conical in shape.

blooms. Beneath these were laid out rectangular beds, each spilling over with a single species of flower in one solid colour – blue *Plumbago larpentae*, pink bergenia, scarlet oriental poppies, lilies, aquilegias and dwarf roses – all edged with purple aubrietia and forming a kaleidoscopic display changing with the seasons.

It was Monet's habit to visit the Clos Normand, inspecting, checking, straightening, altering, removing – nothing escaped his eagle eye. Every morning he consulted the barometer and the thermometer, and at first light he scrutinized the hill opposite for the day's weather forecast, and checked a few tools, which in fact were the same as those he used to paint outdoors. His bravura approach to shaping the garden ensured that – even as he pruned, cut and trained so assiduously – it was never in danger of looking like a stage set or backdrop. The showers of roses, swags of sweet peas, festoons of *Cobaea scandens* and cascades of Russian vine (polygonum) were all apparently so artless. Monet's skill in composing images with everyday common or garden flowers was all down to his gift for creating groups, for making dense associations or loosely scattered plantings in a skilful combination of native species and wild flowers, garden staples and botanical rarities. It was essentially a garden of perennials, highlighted by annuals. Monet established a number of basic principles to which he always adhered: bare earth was anathema to him; he avoided dark flowers; conversely, he could never get enough of blue, so rare in nature; he adored single flowers, permitting double blooms only in roses and herbaceous peonies; and he loathed variegated foliage.

Nothing could be simpler than the list of his favourite basic plants, incomplete as it is, in a happy confusion of annuals, perennials and flowering seasons: eryngium, echinops, cornflowers, all varieties of sunflower, corn poppies, Icelandic poppies, Shirley poppies and poppies of every sort, escholtzia, yellow and white marguerites, verbascum, stocks, sweet rocket, foxgloves, mallows, aquilegias, all campanulas, delphiniums, asters, bugloss, love-in-a-mist, morning glory, sweet peas, epilobium, tree poppies, Solomon's seal, dicentra, phlox, Japanese anemones, aconites, *Nicotiana sylvestris*, tobacco plants, acanthus, hydrangeas and many, many more.

As the seasons unfolded, cushions of crocus, scillas and primulas and drifts of snowdrops gave way to carpets of narcissus and successive waves of tulips, *T. botanica*, Rembrandt and Darwin. Then came pools of *Iris germanica, I. kaempferi, I. reticulata, I. pumila, I. sibirica* and more, with a glorious profusion of peonies, and above all the fragile elegance of tree peonies from China and Japan. Later in the season, these gave way to golden showers of heleniums and sunflowers, with mounds of asters and dahlias by the hundred.

Irises were one of Monet's great passions: Dutch iris, I. kaempferi, I. japonica and I. ochroleuca.

Roses, meanwhile, formed a whole collection of their own, including *R. gallica, R. centifolia* and *R. alba*, noisette and damask, bourbon and tea, climbers and ramblers, shrub and dwarf species. Among the profusion of climbers scrambling up the house, trees and pergolas, "Mermaid", bearing its beautiful large single yellow blooms on the south façade, was Monet's favourite. But all the climbers were spectacular: "Virginie et Perpétue" on the metal pergola, "American Pillar" with its magnificent if once-flowering deep red blooms with white centres sharing a wall with a bignonia. Other roses smothered a variety of arches and other supports: *R. wichuriana*; the beautiful Bourbon rose "Louise Odier"; "Princesse Louise", with fragrant pink globular blooms;

Avenue of Iris germanica

Left:
A bed of tulips in front of the house in spring.

Above:
Spring display of tulips, daffodils and narcissi.

"Madame Isaac Pereire"; the graceful "Madame Alfred Carrière", delicately perfumed and one of the most elegant of the noisettes, perfect for cutting; and "Zéphirine Drouhin" bearing glorious carmine-pink blooms on thornless stems throughout the summer. All Monet's flowers were planted in monochrome blocks of solid colour, carefully juxtaposed and designed to be viewed on the diagonal. Thus the saffron garden leads to the bronze garden, the crimson garden or the mauve garden described by Sacha Guitry, in a conflagration of colour of an intensity that was unprecedented.

In winter, when the dormant terrain was once more revealed in its strict geometry, nothing could be more exotic or soothing than a visit to the hothouse, with its pool of fragile water lilies amid a forest of ferns, the sinuous silver foliage of a tillandsia, stands of sprekelias, tuberoses, strelitzias and other species whose names have been lost, spiky and unkempt, sprouting strange crests, prickles and aerial roots, all so unfamiliar to western eyes. Then there was the mysterious world of epiphytic plants, drawing moisture from the air. Pots suspended from the roof held the intoxicatingly beautiful world of the orchid family: the lovely oncidiums or "dancing ladies", delicate dendrobiums and phalaenopsis, impressively large *Stanhopea tigrina* and – one of the smallest and Monet's favourite – the charming lady's slipper.

For Monet the Clos Normand was an extension of the house, where he liked to receive visitors: its paths and beds offered a generous welcome to all, whether busy dealers in a hurry, such as Durand-Ruel and Bernheim; collectors; children; Japanese friends such as the Kurokis and Mr Hayashi; American artists such as Whistler and Sargent; or French friends, close and not so close, including fellow gardeners. Most of this latter group – including statesmen, politicians, writers, actors, painters, photographers and even film-makers – were city-dwellers. At Giverny, their close empathy with nature and passion for gardens would soothe them of the strains and stresses of urban life, plunging them into a tireless round of country pursuits and incessant, urgent correspondence. Confronted with the enchanted world of plants, they marvelled and despaired: so impossibly exacting, fragile, ephemeral, capricious and (in a word) unreliable was it that it rendered them insatiably restless and curious, constantly prey to delicious but incurable maladies and recurrent torments:

– Still hunting for the parent plant of the sweet lemon tree [*Citrus limetta*] growing beside the boiler room. *Diable*, but there are only some 300 different lemon trees!

– A treacherous early frost has massacred the fluted petals of our cherished dahlia "Etoile de Digoin".

– The enormous stove in the hothouse has a slight cough, so a rest is prescribed: one breakdown and tragedy ensues for all those beautiful exotics.

Above all, this obsessive coterie was condemned to travel the world or beg from all and sundry to get hold of that precious seed or cutting that they had to have at all costs. Mirbeau was beyond question the worst affected. Between his articles in defence of Abbé Bégon and his shamefully reviled begonias, his despairing letters whenever his garden was assailed by rough winds or rain, and his avowed passion for soil and compost, Mirbeau displayed all the symptoms of this malady in its most acute form. "PS Keep a few horned poppy seeds for me. And don't forget my dahlia cuttings, and I won't forget yours!" he wrote to Monet, or, "I have received two roots

A pergola of pink and white Clematis montana in the west garden.

of *Silphium albiflorum*, I shall keep some seeds for you," or again, "Remember to give me two little roots of *Helianthus multiflorus maximus*?" (and other passions to which he confessed in *Le Concombre fugitif*, or "The Fugitive Cucumber'). Not to mention the mania for collecting the entire family of artemisias, or senecios, or whatever, or the tragedy of the rose brought all the way from Pennsylvania that would have to remain anonymous as someone lost the name tag...

Clemenceau was not immune either, with his *gazon de Mahon* and his *boules d'azur*, his railing against the ocean, and his stubborn determination to cultivate a garden on sand when he was already quite seriously ill. To Monet he protested:

> *"What is making my recovery slower is not even having the name of the plant for which I asked you, and being reduced to dithering between agravanose and paremaganase, unless of course it might be geraricondro. Please rescue me from my predicament."*

In among the exasperated neologisms and the deadpan humour, we may perhaps detect the fears of a psychiatrist in the face of the ageing process. For Monet, Mirbeau and their fellow horticultural enthusiasts, the existence of a private world away from the tumult and prying eyes of society, a patch of nature to call one's own, was an absolute necessity.

Caillebotte's gardens at Yerres and Petit-Gennevilliers (Le Casin), Charlotte Lysés and Sacha Guitry's at Yanville, and above all Alice and Octave Mirbeau's Les Damps and Clos Saint-Blaise – all these were responses to this pressing need. For Monet, the Clos Normand, where he was to do so many of his paintings, was absolutely indispensable as his outdoor studio and working tool. With the water garden of which he had been thinking for so long and which he was now about to create, it was his own triumphantly successful response to his driving need to create a contemporary version of the private world of the *hortus conclusus*.

Claude Monet, Yellow and Mauve Irises, *n.d., Musée Marmottan-Monet, Paris.*

Claude Monet, Agapanthus, *Musée Marmottan-Monet, Paris.*

Claude Monet, The Artist's Garden at Giverny, *1900, Musée d'Orsay, Paris.*

The Water Garden and Water Lily Studio

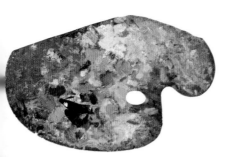

Monet's palette, preserved in the Musée Marmottan-Monet, Paris.

Enlarging the garden, extending it with an expanse of water – this had been Monet's dream from the very start. By now he had been at Giverny barely ten years, and yet what changes he had wrought! Now it was time to move on to the "Meadow". When the railway had arrived in 1860, the embankment work had created a patch of water where a few wild water lilies had happily made themselves at home. Alice for her part had never been able to forget the lake at Montgeron, and for Monet water was like a magnet, its presence an obsession.

Gradually, through a piecemeal process of buying some parcels of land and renting others, Monet managed to acquire ownership of this plot of land. Between 1893 and 1895 he without respite (apart from a trip to Norway) on his *Cathedrals* series on the one hand, and on the excavation of his pond on the other.

The very first pond at Giverny anticipated Monet by several centuries, however, as it was the work of the "farmer monks" attached to the rigorously intellectual abbey of Saint-Ouen at Rouen. It was they who created the Ru in the Middle Ages, as a means of irrigating their stewpond and increasing their stocks of fish. Through their ingenious system of sluice gates, which enabled them to irrigate and flood the rich pastures grazed by their herds, along with their arable fields marbled with wild flowers, they managed to increase both stocks of game in the woods and the harvests from the fields.

The Ru was thus a man-made tributary of the Epte, which flowed ultimately into a branch of the Seine. When, much later, the Compagnie des Chemins de Fer de l'Ouest came to Giverny, it laid the track for its little train parallel not only to the stream but also to the Chemin du Roy, the only road then running through the valley. Monet had other ideas, however. It occurred to him that he could change the course of the Ru, diverting it – only slightly – and creating a bend to feed another pond, this time his own, for his own aesthetic pleasure. A system of sluice gates would return the water to the Ru, naturally. When the local villagers got wind of the plan, however, there was uproar. The municipal council blocked the plan, while some of the villagers raised their own individual objections, though without being required to give any reason. Oddly, local farmers claimed that the livestock that they brought to drink from the Ru twice a day would be endangered, as the water would be polluted by these strange water plants – despite the fact that were actually indigenous species. Two inquiries were ordered, and the whole affair became both tedious and time-consuming.

As a respectable and dutiful citizen, Monet had written on 17 March 1893 to the Prefect of the Eure department:

> *Monsieur le Préfet*
>
> *I have the honour to inform you that I am the owner of a plot of land bounded by Pacy-Gisors railway line and the left bank of a branch of the Epte, and the tenant of the land forming the opposite bank of this branch. In order to replenish the water in the ponds that I intend to excavate on the land that belongs to me with a view to cultivating aquatic plants, I should like to create a water supply from the Epte by means of a small open-ended ditch in the right bank of the Epte, equipped with a small sluice gate, 60 or 70 centimetres wide.*

The wildest corner of the water lily pond, with at the far end the little bridge leading to the sluice gates.

No mechanism would be sited on the river bed to modify either the level or flow of water. In short, this concerns merely a minor and intermittent diversion of an insignificant volume of water in relation to the flow of the river, which would be returned to the main flow after watering my plants. I believe that my plans lie within the rights of riverside landowners.

Although Monet wrote as from Giverny, he was in fact deeply involved at this point in working on his *Cathedrals* series in Rouen. Alice kept him abreast of developments by post, telling him in her letters of the feeling in the village with regard to his pond. In Monet's view this was nothing but an idiotic fuss about nothing, but in the end he lost his temper:

Rouen, Monday evening, second letter of 20 March 1893 to Alice Monet:

I'm distressed by these new difficulties. I was completely absorbed in my painting and relatively pleased. This puts me in a rage and I don't want anything to do with it any more, with these Malassis and all these other people in Giverny, plus the engineers, diggers etc. There is nothing but trouble in store, and ma foi I wash my hands of it. I am not writing to the Préfet. I shall wire Lagrange not to send anything. Don't hire anything, don't order up any wire mesh and throw the aquatic plants in the river, where they'll grow. I want to hear no more about it, I want to paint. Merde to the natives of Giverny, and to the engineers.

Anyone who wants the land is welcome to it. I'm furious, there it is. Forgive me for writing these lines, but I never seem to get any luck, every time I go away to work another problem rears up to claim my attention.

Oh to live on a desert island. Oh well, if I can manage to sleep and paint tomorrow I don't give a fig about the rest.

Following a series of interventions from friends, on 17 July of that year he wrote to the Prefect again:

Japanese maple by the pond.

The walk to the pond.

... I should explain that the cultivation of aquatic plants that I mentioned is not as ambitious a project as it may sound, consisting only of a decorative feature to please the eye, and also to provide motifs for my paintings; and also that I shall only be growing plants such as water lilies, rushes and different varieties of iris, which in the ordinary way grow naturally along the riverbank, and that cannot possibly poison the water...

A week later, on 24 July, the Prefect issued two orders granting the necessary permissions, so finally drawing the affair to a close.

The first pond that Monet dug was rectangular in shape, fairly narrow and straight-edged, and over this he built a single-span bridge of Japanese inspiration. Around this basically rather ordinary feature, he then wove the magic of his vision as gardener. Photographs taken during a visit by the young Joseph Durand-Ruel and his wife in 1898 are striking for the beauty of the scattered mounds of water lilies, for the profusion of trees that have been planted, and for the impression of space created by the little winding paths laid out around the pond. The dense planting was fringed with grasses, and there was a clever contrast between this semi-wilderness and the controlled elegance of the pond. Already the banks are planted with particular attention: if Monet wanted to paint the reflections in the water, he had to take care that the waterside planting should be neither too tall nor too close to the water.

Within three years the scene was ready for him to paint his bridge series, including *The Water Lily Pond, Harmony in Green* and *Harmony in Pink*. And he could not resist painting his first Japanese bridge in a winter frost, a few days before he set off on his trip to Norway. Soon the oval created by the arch of the bridge and its reflection in the water was to captivate him utterly. By 1901 his insatiably curious eye had explored every possible viewpoint; he did not know at this point that he was now inexorably ensnared in a controlling passion that was to bind him to this

The great weeping willow, which appears in the great water lily paintings in the Orangerie.

Reflections between cushions of water lilies, Monet's favourite subject, after the alterations to the pond of 1901.

pond for the rest of his life. Now he decided to enlarge it to encompass virtually the whole of the Meadow, and as the whole area was restructured and planted up with new species, the water garden started to assume an increasingly oriental air. Immense kalmias and clumps of mixed bamboos, some sent by cousins of Alice who had been posted to Indochina, occupied the right-hand side of the pond, where a curved stone bench made a charming spot to sit and listen to the birds that thronged the dense vegetation. The enormous circular leaves of petasites and the sword-shaped foliage of every variety of water iris softened the curves of the banks, and groups of agapanthus, hemerocallis in unusual shades and Japanese tree peonies dotted the immaculate lawns – all conspiring to emphasize the serenity and restraint of this part of the garden, an aesthetic of stillness that inspires contemplation. Monet the painter had discovered another source of inspiration that was to last for at least the next decade.

The Japanese bridge now vanished from his paintings, to reappear only much later, in about 1911, when his sight was already damaged by cataracts. No damage is evident in his paintings, however. These were years that he devoted to painting the surface of the water and all that was reflected in it, a perpetual and never-ending obsession that preoccupied his days, regardless of the season or the weather. Unable to work in the water garden during the major works for this second excavation, Monet set up his easel in the Clos Normand, where he did magnificent paintings of the central path, of the mauve blooms of *Iris pallida*, and of *The House Seen from the Rose Garden* – works that also tracked the progress of the cataracts of which he had recognized the first symptoms in 1908, the year of his visit to Venice.

After the excavation of the pond Monet painted very little at Giverny, in fact, preferring to avoid the crowds of admiring visitors who flocked to see it. Another phase of his life seemed to be opening up now, in which he frequently took off on his travels in the winter in order to paint. When he was a to home he worked in

Wild areas around the pond.

The water lilies were always planted in massed groups.

peace away from the house, often on the Ile des Orties, which he immortalized in his *Morning on the Seine* series, and which sadly disappeared when the channel was widened. He also returned to the Channel coast, to his beloved Pourville, to Varengeville, and even to the dreaded Vétheuil, where he painted a series of views from Lavacourt in 1901. He made frequent trips to London, and also finally – following in the footsteps of all his fellow artists – Venice.

In 1911, he felt a burning need to alter the pond for a third time. Alice's death in that year plunged him into a state of abject despair: profoundly shaken, he gave up painting, declaring that he was finished and that everything he had done was merely second-rate. But the pond underwent new changes: a trellis now covered the Japanese bridge, to be adorned with a purple-flowering Chinese wisteria, followed by a white-flowering Japanese wisteria with long, graceful racemes. The outlines of the landscape were rearranged once more. For a long time Monet had been thinking of painting series or groups of very different canvases. While waiting for this idea to evolve in his mind and find expression through his failing sight, he painted details: numerous studies of wisteria, and of graceful groups of hemerocallis, agapanthus and iris. And he cut "windows" into the growth of the wisterias on the bridge, so that he could paint the view through them and beneath the arch of the bridge.

Though only modest in size, this was a space that was to prove a source of inexhaustible inspiration for Monet, a veritable forest of motifs. The idea for a special series of paintings on a large scale was now taking shape, to stay with him for the rest of his life. And now life – as is so often the way – seemed to assail him with one calamity after another. The crippling blow of Alice's death was followed in 1914 by that of his son Jean. This came shortly after the departure of Marthe and Theodore Butler for America, where Theodore was to finish a mural in one of the enormous mansions springing up in the Hudson valley to house a new breed of wealthy patrons of the arts. With their departure, Monet lost not only the

Groups of iris and caltha (water buttercup) beside the little bridge.

companionship of his grandchildren but also the attentions of Marthe, who since her mother's death had taken on the running of the house. Monet's cataracts were encroaching steadily on his vision War broke out.

The newly widowed Blanche returned to live with Monet and would remain with him to the end, along with his surviving son Michel. But the house that had been filled with the shouts and laughter of children, that had welcomed crowds of friends and witnessed all kinds of entertaining foibles and genial eccentricities, now echoed only to the monotonous daily round of three adults, all of them slightly at a loss.

Though easily discouraged, Monet was equally prompt in picking himself up again, and refused to give up. The idea of painting a large decorative series had taken firm root, and it with this in view that he had already remodelled the water lily pond for the third time. He even decided to build a vast studio specially for the purpose, just a hundred metres from the pond: the water lily pond in its third incarnation, the third studio and the great series of decorative paintings that it was designed to house thus formed one inseparable whole.

Each stage in the development of the water lily pond has its own series of water lily paintings, each marking a different period. Looking at the imposing third studio today, it is hard to imagine that it was built on the site of a derelict house and hen-house above and to the west of the Clos Normand, towards the ruelle l'Amsicourt. Permission to build was granted by the prefecture on 5 July 1915, and no time was lost in setting to work. The structure consisted essentially of a single vast space under a roof that was glazed throughout in order to capture the maximum light, as in nature. A removable awning allowed the light to be filtered to the desired level, and a large door gave access to the garden. Nothing could have been simpler. The large area of wooden floor required the services of a floor-polisher from Vernon, for despite the massive scale of his canvases, the impressive scope of his palette and the spirited nature of his brushwork, Monet was both careful and fastidious. Paul, the cook's husband who stood in for the floor-polisher for a while, maintained that he never saw it stained by a single splash of paint. By the end of 1915, the studio was ready for Monet to use.

There was an element of undeniable if judicious folly in Monet's dogged determination to build this ambitious structure – 15 metres tall, 23 metres long and 12 metres wide – at his age (he was by now seventy-five) and at a time of general mobilization, when all the local able-bodied men had been called up for war service. And even when the building was up it still caused him major problems, as did the business of painting.

Etienne Clémentel, Minister for Trade and Industry, was a valuable friend and ally who helped Monet tremendously during the war years, intervening when his car was requisitioned, and finding him petrol and cigarettes. On one occasion Monet wrote to thank him "for the coal"; on another to inform him in panic-stricken tones that "something terrible has befallen me, my paint merchant has run out of oil and cannot supply me any more"; on a third he begged a favour: "that the railway should transport my large easels and canvases as express freight". Everything was

The Japanese bridge, with one of the wisterias.

a problem, even finding carpenters to make crates for his paintings so that he could send them to dealers.

A letter that Monet wrote after the war to Clémentel, who had become senator for the Puy-de-Dôme region, indicates the voracious appetite of the large stove: "how can I get supplies of coal to heat my studio… I need ten tonnes." Thadée Natanson has left the following evocative description of the paintings that were the fruit of all these labours:

> There is one visit to Monet at Giverny, one late summer's afternoon, that I am sure that neither Bonnard nor Ker Roussel nor Vuillard will ever have forgotten. Monet had invited us all together to view the Water Lily paintings, which were nearly all finished, but of which we had only been allowed glimpses some of the earliest in the series. In the immense studio that the artist had built for them at the bottom of the garden, he and his daughter-in-law sat us down and then, holding at arm's length canvases as tall as a man – as now in the gallery – moved them around and changed the order of them, gradually surrounding us with one circle of paintings and then with another. Between them these circles included virtually all of the paintings now displayed in the two galleries of the Orangerie. Monet never saw the paintings hung in situ, but already he carried their precise arrangement in his head.

> Thadée Natanson

Claude Monet, Lily Butler and Madame Kuroki, 1921.

Monet painted prolifically in the great water lily studio. But his intention to donate this series to the state in commemoration of the Armistice, which had obsessed him for so long and for which he had attempted the impossible, was to encounter

Claude Monet, Water Lilies, Musée Marmottan-Monet, Paris, 1903.

Georges Clemenceau, Claude Monet and Lily Butler, 1921.

innumerable problems, and Clémentel had to step in to take charge of negotiations with Paul Léon, Minister for the Beaux-Arts. Monet was hard to please. To exhibit his water lily paintings he was offered the gardens of the Hôtel de Biron, which proved impossible, then the Jeu de Paume, and finally the Orangerie. On 31 October 1921, Monet wrote to Clemenceau:

It is to be understood, firstly, that I refuse the offer of the galleries of the Jeu de Paume, and that I do so formally. But I accept the galleries of the Orangerie, on condition that the Beaux-Arts administration undertakes to carry out the works that I judge to be indispensable. With this possibility in mind, I have reduced several subjects of the Decorations and believe I have arrived at an arrangement that would give a happy result while retaining the oval shape that I have always wanted. Instead of the 12 panels that I have given, I shall give 18. It is true that the number is of little account in this matter, but only the quality, and I myself no longer know what to think of this work. The main thing is that it should be well displayed, and I believe that on considered reflection I have arrived at a good result. I am sending you herewith a plan showing roughly what I would like: a first one of which you were able to judge the effect yesterday, and a second of which the key element would be the background formed of the four panels of the Three Willows and opposite them the Reflections of Trees, with a six-metre panel on each side.

If the administration accepts this proposition and undertakes to do the necessary works, then the matter is settled.

It was Clemenceau, again, who realized that Monet was sinking into the increasing darkness caused by his cataracts, which were growing worse but for which he

Claude Monet, Water Lilies, *1916-19,* Musée Marmottan-Monet, Paris.

dreaded seeking treatment. Ever the doctor figure in their long friendship, he now intervened to care for his dear "dauber" friend's psyche, urging that Monet should no longer touch certain parts of his work, as he risked damaging them beyond repair. In 1923, Dr Coutela operated on Monet's cataracts.

So low had Monet's spirits sunk that he even considered the devastating possibility of going back on the whole idea of the donation and compensating the state for the loss. Clemenceau wrote to Blanche with his implacable response: if Monet could not be persuaded to see reason, Clemenceau would never see him again. As he protested to Monet: "there can be no "ifs" in the commitments that you have made".

Thus rebuked in the strongest possible terms, Monet revoked his desperate decision, and all – or nearly all – returned to the status quo. The terms of the donation were agreed and signed at Vernon, but the paintings were not to leave Giverny in Monet's lifetime. Clemenceau, himself exhausted and gravely ill, understood how difficult it was for Monet to part from them, and obtained permission for them to stay with him.

Enriched by Monet's donation, the Orangerie was officially opened in 1927. While being a true reflection of their times, the architect Camille Lefèvre's designs, also achieved a truly symbiotic relationship with the arrangement and juxtapositions of a the paintings – worked out down to the smallest detail by Monet himself, in discreet homage to the Japanese print. Wherever visitors to the Orangerie may come from, from Buenos, Aires, New York or St Petersburg, they are touched by Monet's vision. From this plot of land between the Epte, the Ru and the Seine, Monet created a place that – in its decorative power, its symmetries that are never found in nature, and its elegant synthesis – is timeless, dateless and universal. Some may claim that the *Grandes Décorations* are the negation of the subject in painting. Do they not rather re-create the essential subject that has escaped out gaze?

The Water Lily Studio in the 1920s. Here Monet was able to arrange his paintings as he wanted to see them displayed at the Orangerie.

Claude Monet, The Water Lily Pond: Harmony in Green, *1899, Musée d'Orsay, Paris.*

Claude Monet, Water Lilies: Evening Effect, 1897-8, Musée Marmottan-Monet, Paris.

The Hoschedé-Monet family

Halfway up the hillside stands the church of Sainte Radegonde, touching in its Romanesque simplicity. Behind it, in 1891, Monet and Alice chose a spot overlooking the apse, where all the family would be buried.

The first to be interred in this burial plot belonging to the Hoschedé family was the patron of art Ernest Hoschedé. He was followed by Suzanne Hoschedé-Butler, Monet's model for *Woman with a Parasol*; a Hoschedé-Salerou granddaughter who died in childhood; Alice Hoschedé-Monet in 1911; Jean Monet in 1914; Claude Monet himself in 1926; the artist Blanche Hoschedé-Monet in 1947; and Gabrielle Bonaventure-Monet and her husband Michel Monet in 1966. Michel, Monet's younger son, bequeathed his entire estate to the Académie des beaux-arts de l'Institut de France.

The grave is a square garden filled with successive seasonal plantings of flowers surrounded by horizontal white marble plaques bearing the names of those buried there. From 1891 until his death, Monet was able to consider how he wanted his last resting place to be; he did not want a mausoleum.

The artist had refused both the Légion d'Honneur and a seat at the Institut. Disliking ostentation in any form, he did not want a state funeral, preferring a private ceremony with as few people present as possible. Jean-Pierre Hoschedé was instructed to telephone the Prefect to ask him to ensure that no speeches or eulogies were given. Monet was carried to his final resting place, in this land that he had so loved and celebrated, in the Charitons' handcart, like any local villager. Behind the cart walked family members, a few friends and the people of Giverny. His last wishes were followed to the letter. In the cemetery stood Clemenceau, waiting for the funeral procession of his old friend.

The grave of Claude Monet at Giverny. Photography: J-M Peers de N. Reproduced by permission of the Hoschedé-Monet family.

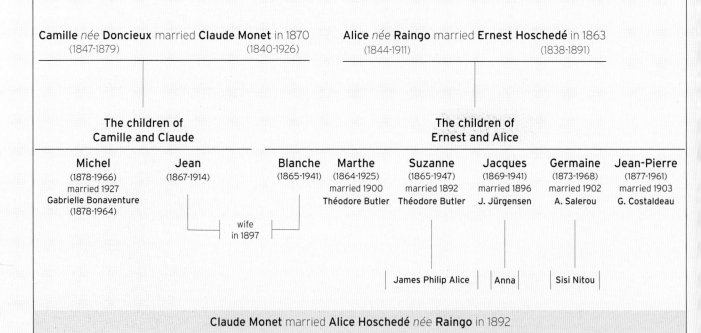

Camille *née* **Doncieux** married **Claude Monet** in 1870
(1847-1879)   (1840-1926)

Alice *née* **Raingo** married **Ernest Hoschedé** in 1863
(1844-1911)   (1838-1891)

The children of
Camille and Claude

The children of
Ernest and Alice

Michel	**Jean**	**Blanche**	**Marthe**	**Suzanne**	**Jacques**	**Germaine**	**Jean-Pierre**
(1878-1966)	(1867-1914)	(1865-1941)	(1864-1925)	(1865-1947)	(1869-1941)	(1873-1968)	(1877-1961)
married 1927			married 1900	married 1892	married 1896	married 1902	married 1903
Gabrielle Bonaventure			Théodore Butler	Théodore Butler	J. Jürgensen	A. Salerou	G. Costaldeau
(1878-1964)							

wife in 1897

James Philip Alice   Anna   Sisi Nitou

Claude Monet married **Alice Hoschedé** *née* **Raingo** in 1892

Chronology

1840
Oscar-Claude Monet born in Paris
on 14 November.

c.1845
The Monet family moves to Le Havre.

c.1856-8
Monet starts to gain a reputation as a
caricaturist; he meets Boudin, who introduces
him to painting.

1858
Submits a painting to the Exposition Municipale
in Le Havre. With the help of his family he goes
to Paris, where Amand Gautier introduces him
to Troyon and the Realist circle. Attends the
Académie Suisse, where he probably meets
Pissarro.

1861-2
Military service in Algeria. On returning to
Le Havre meets Jongkind in the autumn of 1862.

1862-3
Monet enters the studio of Gleyre in Paris,
where he becomes friends with Bazille,
Renoir and probably Sisley.

1864
Stays in Honfleur with Bazille, then with Boudin
and Jongkind. Experiences difficulties with
his family.

1865
Two landscapes accepted at the Paris Salon;
starts work on his *Déjeuner sur l'herbe*,
which is almost finished by the end of the year.
Courbet congratulates him on this work.

1866
Leaves *Déjeuner sur l'herbe* unfinished; is
successful at the Salon with *Camille*, which Zola
particularly admires; meets Manet; moves to
Sèvres, where he paints *Women in the Garden*,
then goes to Honfleur; beset by financial
difficulties.

1867
Lives with Bazille at 20, rue Visconti; *Women
in the Garden* refused by the Salon; moves
to Sainte-Adresse; his future wife, Camille
Doncieux, gives birth to their first child, Jean.

1868
One painting accepted at the Salon; continuing
financial difficulties are helped by the Gaudiberts,
art lovers from Le Havre; awarded a gold medal
at the 'Maritime International Exhibition'
at Le Havre (October).

1869
Refused by the Salon; moves to Saint-Michel,
near Bougival, where he works alongside Renoir;
also paints at Louveciennes with Pissarro.

1870
Refused by the Salon; marries Camille Doncieux;
following the outbreak of the Franco-Prussian
war, takes refuge in England with his family
in the summer.

1870-1
In London, meets Pissarro again and also
the art dealer Paul Durand-Ruel; travels
to Zaandam, Holland, then back to France,
where in late 1871 he settles at Argenteuil.

1872
Spends time in Rouen and Le Havre;
also works in Argenteuil.

1874
First exhibition of the Société Anonyme des
Artiste, in which Monet shows the painting
Impression, Sunrise, the origin of the term
"Impressionism".

1876
Takes part in the second "Impressionist
Exhibition", notably with landscapes of Argenteuil
and *La Japonaise*; paints decorative panels
for Ernest and Alice Hoschédé at their chateau
of Rottembourg at Montgeron.

1877
Works on views of the *Gare Saint-Lazare*,
some of which he shows at the third
"Impressionist Exhibition".

1878
Forced to leave Argenteuil at the beginning of the
year, moves temporarily to 26, rue d'Edimbourg
in Paris, where his second son, Michel, is born;
soon afterwards, moves to Vétheuil.

1879
Shows twenty-nine works at the fourth
Impressionist Exhibition, now the Salon des
Artistes Indépendants (at 28, avenue de l'Opéra,
10 April to 11 May). Death of Camille Monet
on 5 September.

1880
Inspired by the breaking up of ice on the
Seine in early January, Monet paints several
spectacular paintings. With a large landscape
of Lavacourt, he is accepted at the Salon (opens
1 May) and also takes part in the fifth Salon
des Artistes Indépendants. First solo exhibition
(of eighteen paintings) on the premises of
the review *La Vie Moderne* (opens 7 June).
Sends a few works, including the Salon painting,
to the Exposition de la Société des Amis
des Arts in Le Havre (August). While staying
at his brother's home in Rouen, visits
Les Petites-Dalles on the Normandy coast.

1881
From 17 February, Durand-Ruel makes regular
purchases of Monet's work; Monet paints at
Fécamp (March to April), then Trouville and
Sainte-Adresse (September); moves with Alice
Hoschédé and children to the Villa Saint-Louis
in Poissy (December).

1882
After a few days in Dieppe, paints at Pourville,
where he stays at A la Renommée des Galettes
(15 February to mid-April). Shows thirty-five
works at the seventh Salon des Artistes
Indépendants at the Panorama de Reichshoffen
(251, rue Saint Honoré) in March, held in aid
of Durand-Ruel, badly affected financially
by the crash of the Union Générale (February).
In summer, stays with Alice and children at
the Villa Juliette in Pourville (June), before
returning to Poissy (5 October) after a short
stay in Rouen; carries out decorative paintings
for salon of Durand-Ruel's apartment
(35, rue de Rome), on which he will continue
working until 1885.

1883
Spends a few days in Le Havre, then on to
the Hôtel Blanquet in Etretat (late January

to 21 February); Durand-Ruel organizes a solo
exhibition of fifty-six of Monet's works (March).
Monet stays at Giverny with Alice Hoschédé
and their children (April). During second
fortnight of December, travels with Renoir along
Mediterranean coast to Genoa. They meet
Cézanne in Aix-en Provence.

1884
Stays in Bordighera on the Riviera du Ponant,
then in Menton (January to mid-April).
Goes to Etretat (August).

1885
Takes part for the first time in the Exposition
Internationale organized by the art dealer
Georges Petit (opens 15 May at 8, rue de Sèze).
Settles in Etretat with Alice and children in
house lent by the singer Faure (mid-September).
Alone from 10 October, boards at the Hôtel
Blanquet until mid-December, often meeting
Maupassant.

1886
Returns to Etretat (February) and sends ten works
to the Exposition des XX in Brussels (February);
Durand-Ruel exhibits some forty paintings by
Monet at the exhibition *Works in Oil and Pastel
by the Paris Impressionists* in New York (April
to May). Monet spends ten days in Holland
(27 April to 6 May) as the guest of Baron
D'Estournells de Constant, Secretary to the
Embassy of the French Legation in The Hague.
Takes part in the fifth Exposition Internationale
at the Galerie Petit (opens 15 June). Stays at
Belle-Ile (September to November), where he
meets Gustave Geffroy, art critic of *La Justice*;
ends his trip to Brittany with a visit to Octave
Mirbeau at Noirmoutier (late November).

1887
Takes part in the sixth Exposition Internationale
at the Galerie Petit (8 May to 8 June); short stay
in London (August); thanks to Whistler, shows
at the exhibition of the Royal Society of British
Artists (November).

1888
Works in Antibes and Juan-les-Pins (mid-January
to early May); at Antibes stays – at the same
time as the painter Harpignies – at the Château
de la Pinède, an artists' retreat recommended
by Maupassant, whom he has met in Cannes.
At 19, boulevard Montmartre (June), Théo
van Gogh exhibits the ten 'Antibes seascapes'
(as Félix Fénéon called them) bought from
Monet by him on behalf of the Boussod-Valadon
Gallery. Monet makes a short trip to London
(July).

1889
Geffroy takes Monet, Louis Mullern and Frantz
Jourdain to spend a few days in the Vallée de
la Creuse, where they visit the poet Maurice
Rollinat in Fresselines (second fortnight of
February); enthusiastic about the region, Monet
returns to stay there from March to mid-May.
'Monet-Rodin' exhibition at the Galerie Petit
(June); three works shown, along with Manet's
Olympia, at the Exposition Centennale de l'Art
Français, which opens in May, at the same time
as the Exposition Universelle; Monet starts a
fund in order to present *Olympia* to the Louvre;
after a hard-fought campaign, he persuades
to accept the painting in 1890 for the Musée
du Luxembourg.

1890

Monet acquires the house and garden in Giverny, where he builds a new studio and works on the garden (autumn).

1891

Fifteen paintings from the *Haystacks* series are shown at the exhibition of "Recent works by Cl. Monet" at the Durand-Ruel Gallery (4-16 May).

1892

Durand-Ruel exhibits some fifteen paintings from the *Poplars* series (29 February to 10 March); Monet stays in Rouen, where he paints the *Cathedrals* series (February to mid-April); in July he marries Alice Hoschédé (Ernest Hoschédé died in March 1891). Monet is refused a decoration at the Hôtel de Ville de Paris (November).

1893

Continues working in Rouen on the *Cathedrals* series (February to mid-April). Buys a plot of land to the south of his house in Giverny (5 February), where he starts excavations for the famous water lily pond and water garden.

1894

Cézanne visits Giverny, where Monet arranges a meeting with Geffroy, Rodin and Clemenceau (28 November).

1895

Trip to Norway (late January to early April); Durand-Ruel devotes an exhibition to Monet (10-31 May) including twenty of the *Cathédrales* series among other works.

1896

Works at Pourville and Varengeville (mid-February to April).

1897

Returns to Pourville and Varengeville (mid-January to March).

1898

Georges Petit stages an exhibition of Monet's most recent works (opens 1 June), featuring notably the *Morning on the Seine* paintings.

1899

Stays in London (autumn).

1900

Returns to London (February). With some recent paintings, about ten versions of the *Water Lily Pond* are shown at the Durand-Ruel Gallery in Paris (22 November to 15 December).

1901

Durand-Ruel stages a similar show in New York (February). Monet stays in London (February to April).

1902

Six *Views of Vétheuil* painted by Monet during the summer of 1900 are unveiled to the public in a joint exhibition with Pissarro's recent work, *Œuvres Récéntes de Pissarro et Nouvelle Série de Monet (Vétheuil)*, at the Bernheim-Jeune Gallery (20 to 28 February).

1904

Thirty-seven *Views of the Thames in London* (1900-4) form the theme of an exhibition at the Durand-Ruel Gallery (9 May to 4 June). Monet visits Madrid to see the works of Velasquez (October); this is followed by a trip to London (December).

1908

Stays in Venice (October to December).

1909

The exhibition *Les Nymphéas, Série de paysages d'eau*, comprising forty-eight works, takes place at the Durand-Ruel Gallery (6 May to 5 June). Monet may have returned to Venice (this is disputed by several authors).

1911

Death of Alice Monet on 19 May.

1912

The Bernheim-Jeune Gallery shows twenty-nine *Views of Venice* (28 May to 8 June).

1914

Monet's elder son, Jean, who married Blanche Hoschédé in June 1897, dies prematurely on 10 February. Monet commissions a special studio, to be finished in 1916, in order to work on his large-scale *Water Lily* paintings.

1922

On 12 April the act of donation of the *Water Lilies* panels to the state is signed, so ratifying Monet's promise to Clemenceau after the 1918 Armistice.

1923

Monet undergoes a cataract operation (his sight had been affected since 1908 and cataracts were diagnosed in 1912).

1924

Durand-Ruel exhibits some of the *Water Lilies* in New York (February).

1926

Vuillard and Roussel visit Monet at Giverny (8 June). Monet dies, aged eighty-six, on 5 December.

Reproduced from Monet au Musée d'Orsay *by Sylvie Patin, Paris, RMN, 2004, by kind permission of Madame Sylvie Patin.*

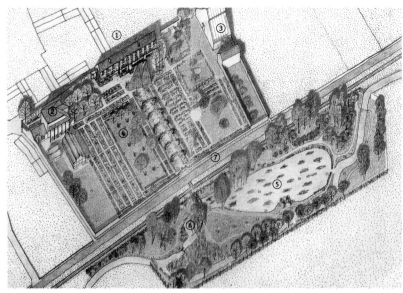

© J.M. Toulgouat

Map of Giverny

① House and first studio
② Second studio
③ Third studio, known as the Water Lily Studio
④ Clos Normand
⑤ Water Lily Pond
⑥ Japanese Bridge
⑦ Chemin du Roy

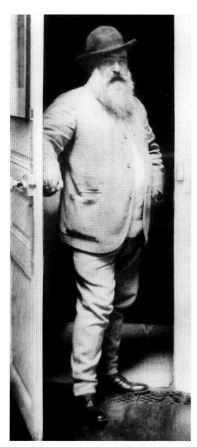

Claude Monet at the threshold of his second studio, 1905.

Fondation Claude Monet
Maison et Jardins de Claude Monet
84, rue Claude-Monet
27620 Giverny France
Tel.: 0033 (0) 2 32 51 28 21
Fax: 0033 (0) 2 32 51 54 18
www.fondation-monet.com
contact@fondation-monet.com

Director:
Monsieur Hugues R. Gall,
Membre de l'Institut

The Fondation is open daily
from 1 April to 1 November
from 9.30am to 6.00pm
(last admission 5.30pm).

Winter closing from
2 November to 31 March.
Information and reservations:
monday to friday, 9.00am–5pm.

Individual visits
Avoid queuing by buying tickets
on www.fondation-monet.com
Advance reservation is not available.

Access by train
SNCF line Paris (Gare Saint-Lazare-Rouen),
alight at Vernon station.

Groups
Advance reservation is obligatory
for groups of 20 or more.
Information and group reservations:
Tel.: 0033 (0) 2 32 51 90 31
Fax: 0033 (0) 2 32 51 91 32
maguero@fondation-monet.co

Average time to allow for visiting
the house and gardens: 2 hours (approx.).
Pets not admitted. Free parking.

Shop
Water Lily Studio
Open daily from 1 April to 1 November,
9.30am–6.15pm.

For purchases by post, please contact us.

The Fondation Claude Monet is owned
by the Académie des Beaux-Arts
(one of the five academies of
the Institut de France).
www.academie-des-beaux-arts.fr

**The Monet Marmottan Garden
in the village of Kitagawa**
In 2000, the Japanese village of Kitagawa-
mura, the Fondation Claude Monet and
the Académie des Beaux-Arts created
the Monet Marmottan Garden, inspired
by Monet's garden at Giverny. The garden
is 90 km from Kochi City, 30 minutes
by air from Osaka and one hour
by air from Tokyo.
www.kjmonet.jp

Restaurant *Les Nymphéas*
Open daily from 1 April to 1 November.
The restaurant lies opposite the exit
from the Fondation Claude Monet
and has free parking.

109, rue Claude-Monet
27620 Giverny
Tel.: 0033 (0) 2 32 21 20 31
Fax: 0033 (0) 2 32 51 15 75
nympheas.giverny@neuf.fr

Graineterie - Flower Shop
Open daily from 1 April to 1 November.
The boutique lies opposite the exit
from the Fondation Claude Monet
and has free parking.
109, rue Claude-Monet
27620 Giverny
Tél. : 02 32 51 99 71

Donations and sponsorship
The restoration of Claude Monet's house
and gardens has been made possible
by the support of many generous patrons
in both France and the United States.
Private individuals and corporations may
contribute to the upkeep of the house
and gardens at Giverny by sending
donations to:
Académie des beaux-arts
Pour la Fondation Claude Monet
23, quai de Conti
75270 Paris Cedex 06
France
Tel. 0033 (0) 1 44 41 43 2
www.academie-des-beaux-arts.fr

For French taxpayers these gifts
are tax-deductible.
(Article 200,23810, 885-0/10
du Code Général des impôts.)

The Versailles Foundation Inc.
Claude Monet-Giverny is a
non-profit-making foundation under
American law which receives tax-exempt
donations and bequests from US
taxpayers:

Donate to address:
The Versailles Foundation Inc.
Claude Monet-Giverny
Fondation Claude Monet
420 Lexington Avenue. Suite 2805
New York City, N.Y. 10170
Tél. : (212) 983-3436
vergivinc@aol.com

*Claude Monet photographed
by Baron Meyer,
27 October 1905.*

Photographic acknowledgments:

Cover photographs: © Fondation Claude Monet, Aude Cauderlier.
Page 2 : © Nickolas Muray, Clemenceau Museum.
Pages 4, 6, 7, 10-1, 12-3 top, 19, 47 top, 70 top, 71 top, 72 low, 79, 80 : Private Collection, DR.
Pages 8, 9, 12, 13, 22, 32, 33, 34-5, 56-7, 61, 70 low, 71 low, 74-5 : © Fondation Claude Monet.
Pages 14, 16-18, 20, 23, 37-9, 40-6, 48-9, 50-3, 60, 62-5, 66 top, 67, 68-9 :
© Fondation Claude Monet, Aude Cauderlier.
Pages 15, 21, 24-31, 36, 47 low, 54-5, 66 low : © Fondation Claude Monet, Jean-Marie del Moral.
Pages 58-9, 73 : © RMN, musée d'Orsay, Hervé Lewandowski.
Page 76 : © J-M Peers de N. Reproduced by permission of the Hoschedé-Monet family.
Page 78 : Planning and design J.-M. Toulgouat. Private Collection, DR.

Produced by Papier and Co
for the Fondation Claude Monet and Editions Gourcuff Gradenigo.

Translated by Barbara Mellor.

Printed in March 2010 by Stipa, Montreuil (Seine-Saint-Denis).

ISBN 978-2-35340-076-8 - French
ISBN 978-2-35340-080-5 - English
ISBN 978-2-35340-081-2 - German
ISBN 978-2-35340-082-9 - Japanese
Legal deposit: 1st quarter 2010
© 2010, Gourcuff Gradenigo – 8, rue des Lilas – 93100 Montreuil
www.gourcuff-gradenigo.com
© 2010, Fondation Claude Monet, Giverny – 84, rue Claude-Monet – 27620 Giverny
www.fondation-monet.com